Bentley College
Waltham, Massachusetts

Written by Jessica Low

Edited by Adam Burns, Matt Hamman, Kimberly Moore, and Jon Skindzier

Layout by Meryl Sustarsic

Additional contributions by Omid Gohari, Christina Koshzow, Chris Mason, Joey Rahimi, and Luke Skurman

ISBN # 1-4274-0022-9
ISSN # 1551-952x
© Copyright 2006 College Prowler
All Rights Reserved
Printed in the U.S.A.
www.collegeprowler.com

Last updated 5/13/06

Special Thanks To: Babs Carryer, Andy Hannah, LaunchCyte, Tim O'Brien, Bob Sehlinger, Thomas Emerson, Andrew Skurman, Barbara Skurman, Bert Mann, Dave Lehman, Daniel Fayock, Chris Babyak, The Donald H. Jones Center for Entrepreneurship, Terry Slease, Jerry McGinnis, Bill Ecenberger, Idie McGinty, Kyle Russell, Jacque Zaremba, Larry Winderbaum, Roland Allen, Jon Reider, Team Evankovich, Lauren Varacalli, Abu Noaman, Mark Exler, Daniel Steinmeyer, Jared Cohon, Gabriela Oates, David Koegler, Glen Meakem, and the Bentley College Bounce-Back Team.

College Prowler®
5001 Baum Blvd.
Suite 750
Pittsburgh, PA 15213

Phone: 1-800-290-2682
Fax: 1-800-772-4972
E-Mail: info@collegeprowler.com
Web Site: www.collegeprowler.com

Welcome to College Prowler®

During the writing of College Prowler's guidebooks, we felt it was critical that our content was unbiased and unaffiliated with any college or university. We think it's important that our readers get honest information and a realistic impression of the student opinions on any campus—that's why if any aspect of a particular school is terrible, we (unlike a campus brochure) intend to publish it. While we do keep an eye out for the occasional extremist—the cheerleader or the cynic—we take pride in letting the students tell it like it is. We strive to create a book that's as representative as possible of each particular campus. Our books cover both the good and the bad, and whether the survey responses point to recurring trends or a variation in opinion, these sentiments are directly and proportionally expressed through our guides.

College Prowler guidebooks are in the hands of students throughout the entire process of their creation. Because you can't make student-written guides without the students, we have students at each campus who help write, randomly survey their peers, edit, layout, and perform accuracy checks on every book that we publish. From the very beginning, student writers gather the most up-to-date stats, facts, and inside information on their colleges. They fill each section with student quotes and summarize the findings in editorial reviews. In addition, each school receives a collection of letter grades (A through F) that reflect student opinion and help to represent contentment, prominence, or satisfaction for each of our 20 specific categories. Just as in grade school, the higher the mark the more content, more prominent, or more satisfied the students are with the particular category.

Once a book is written, additional students serve as editors and check for accuracy even more extensively. Our bounce-back team—a group of randomly selected students who have no involvement with the project—are asked to read over the material in order to help ensure that the book accurately expresses every aspect of the university and its students. This same process is applied to the 200-plus schools College Prowler currently covers. Each book is the result of endless student contributions, hundreds of pages of research and writing, and countless hours of hard work. All of this has led to the creation of a student information network that stretches across the nation to every school that we cover. It's no easy accomplishment, but it's the reason that our guides are such a great resource.

When reading our books and looking at our grades, keep in mind that every college is different and that the students who make up each school are not uniform—as a result, it is important to assess schools on a case-by-case basis. Because it's impossible to summarize an entire school with a single number or description, each book provides a dialogue, not a decision, that's made up of 20 different topics and hundreds of student quotes. In the end, we hope that this guide will serve as a valuable tool in your college selection process. Enjoy!

OMID GOHARI ◯ CHRISTINA KOSHZOW ◯ CHRIS MASON ◯ JOEY RAHIMI ◯ LUKE SKURMAN ◯
The College Prowler Team

Table of Contents

Introduction from the Author

When I was a senior in high school beginning my college search, I had some strict criteria. For one, I wanted a medium-size school close to a major city. Secondly, my school had to have an excellent academic reputation that would prepare me for the business world while also providing a nurturing college environment. Alright, so maybe I was downright picky. My anal-retentive guidance counselor told me I was setting my sights too high and that I would eventually have to settle for a school with only a few of those characteristics because my dream school didn't exist. He was quite wrong.

I found Bentley to be everything I wanted, but I was skeptical because it seemed too good to be true. It only took a short amount of time to realize that Bentley is the real deal: a true business school for the information age. In many ways, the secret is out about Bentley. Since the shift back in the mid-80s away from being a commuter- and accounting-focused school, the school has experienced amazing growth and gained enormous respect within the academic community. I am continually amazed with the academic level in which Bentley contends, as is evident by the increasingly difficult admission criteria. Each class that enters Bentley is more elite than the former, and this is a trend that is expected to continue.

Throughout my years at Bentley, the school underwent a lot of physical changes, from the construction of the state-of-the-art student and technology centers, to building new dorms to fit the growing population. Although the school may look different from when I first toured it, it still has the same feeling of being in an intimate, close-knit community where each student still matters.

While choosing the right college is a personal decision, I believe you should have the right tools available in order to make that decision as informed and educated as possible. This guide is not intended to sway you to attend Bentley; rather, it is the tool you need to gain an insider's perspective on what life is really like at Bentley. At the very least, it should serve you more effectively than your run-of-the-mill high school guidance counselor.

Jessica Low, Author
Bentley College

By the Numbers

General Information

Bentley College
175 Forest Street
Waltham, MA 02452

Control:
Private

Academic Calendar:
Semester

Religious Affiliation:
None

Founded:
1917

Web Site:
www.bentley.edu

Main Phone:
(781) 891-2000

Admissions Phone:
(781) 891-2244

Student Body

**Full-Time
Undergraduates:**
3,919

**Part-Time
Undergraduates:**
338

**Total Male
Undergraduates:**
2,496

**Total Female
Undergraduates:**
1,761

Admissions

Overall Acceptance Rate:
45%

**Early Decision
Acceptance Rate:**
63%

Regular Acceptance Rate:
37%

Total Applicants:
5,865

Total Acceptances:
2,612

Freshman Enrollment:
939

**Yield (% of admitted
students who actually enroll):**
36%

Early Decision Available?
Yes

Early Decision Deadline:
November 15

**Early Decision
Notification:**
December 27

Regular Decision Deadline:
February 1

**Regular Decision
Notification:**
April 1

Must-Reply-By Date:
May 1

**Applicants Placed on
Waiting List:**
936

**Applicants Accepted from
Waiting List:**
770

**Students Enrolled from
Waiting List:**
21

**Transfer Applications
Received:**
460

**Transfer Applications
Accepted:**
256

Transfer Students Enrolled:
154

Transfer Acceptance Rate:
55%

**Common Application
Accepted?**
Yes

→

Supplemental Forms?
Yes

Admissions E-Mail:
ugadmission@bentley.edu

Admissions Web Site:
www.bentley.edu/admission

SAT I or ACT Required?
Either

**SAT I Range
(25th–75th Percentile):**
1120–1280

**SAT I Verbal Range
(25th–75th Percentile):**
580–660

**SAT I Math Range
(25th–75th Percentile):**
570–660

Retention Rate:
94%

**Top 10% of
High School Class:**
35%

Application Fee:
$50

Financial Information

Full-Time Tuition:
$26,824

Room and Board:
$10,170

Books and Supplies:
$960

**Average Need-Based
Financial Aid Package
(including loans, work-study,
grants, and other sources):**
$23,198

**Students Who
Applied For Financial Aid:**
65%

Students Who Received Aid:
36%

Financial Aid Forms Deadline:
February 1

Financial Aid Phone:
(781) 891-3441

Financial Aid E-Mail:
finaid@bentley.edu

Financial Aid Web Site:
*http://ecampus.bentley.edu/
dept/fin*

Academics

The Lowdown On...
Academics

Degrees Awarded:
Associate
Transfer Associate
Terminal Associate
Bachelor
Post-Bachelor Certificate
Master
Post-Master Certificate

Most Popular Majors:
23% Finance
18% Marketing
14% Business
12% Accounting
 8% Computer and
     Information Sciences

Full-Time Faculty:
265

Student-to-Faculty Ratio:
13:1

Faculty with Terminal Degree:
84%

Graduation Rates:
Four-Year: 67%
Five-Year: 75%
Six-Year: 77%

Special Degree Options
Five-year bachelor/master program

AP Test Score Requirements
Possible credit for scores of 3 and higher

Sample Academic Clubs
Bentley Adamian Law Club, Bentley Investment Group, Bentley Marketing Association, Economics and Finance Society, National Association of Black Accountants

Best Places to Study
Dorm study rooms, library, Smith Center, student center

Did You Know?

Each semester, on the night of the last day of classes, students will celebrate the beginning of finals with food, music, and fun during "**Breakfast by Moonlight.**"

Students Speak Out On...
Academics

> **"Teachers are knowledgeable and always willing to help you whenever possible. Most classes are interesting, and professors often share their real-life experience."**

Q "The **teachers are decent**, but every teacher varies. I haven't had one that was terribly bad or extremely good. My classes so far aren't really all that interesting, but I think that's because I am a freshman and am taking filler courses instead of classes related to my major."

Q "Most teachers are great. They know what they are doing, and **they try to make classes as interesting as possible**, but some succeed more than others."

Q "All **professors are more than willing to meet with you** and help you if you need it. The classes are interesting. With tons of elective choices, you can pick classes that are interesting to you."

Q "**The core curriculum is great** because it gives you some background in liberal arts and several aspects of business. Most of my teachers have been great and are very accessible, although, I've had a couple of duds that made me wonder why they were hired."

Q "Overall, **the teachers have good knowledge of topics**. Some teachers are better than others at teaching. You have to do a lot of reading in order to get the most out of class."

Q "I've had all good experiences with the teaching staff here at Bentley. I find them all very reasonable and supportive. **Some of the classes have been boring** from time to time, but since you can pick the topics of most of your classes, its kind of up to you."

Q "The teachers range from extremely interesting to downright boring, just like any other college. However, in my experience, **I have not had a bad teacher** that didn't end up growing on me after a while."

Q "During freshman and sophomore year, the professors are not that good; oftentimes, they are young and inexperienced. However, **the professors in junior and senior year are excellent**. They really build relationships with their students."

Q "I find that **many of my professors do little or nothing to get students involved** in the classroom. With the exception of my GB classes, professors just lecture for an hour and 15 minutes, and then the students get up and leave. Classes are very boring, which causes little or no interest in the coursework and makes college feel like an extension of high school."

Q "**The honors teachers are better** than regular teachers. It seems like all law and psychology teachers are practicing in their profession, which is definitely a good thing because they have anecdotes and personal experiences which increase my understanding of the subject matter."

Q "**Some classes are interesting**, and most of the faculty are very well versed in business; hearing about their experiences can be very beneficial. The general education classes are a little boring, subject-matter wise, but taking them is unavoidable."

Q "Most **professors give a fair workload** and are willing to go out of their way to help you if you ask."

Q "**The professors are great** and easy to talk to. They all basically hold PhDs and are very intelligent. Most work in the business world, so they can relate to you and give you great real-world tips. They are as interesting as classes can get."

Q "The teachers are widely varied in both expertise and teaching ability, but **you will never get a bad teacher** for a class in your major. Bentley just does not allow it."

Q "Some teachers are definitely cool, but **some almost seem too smart**, and it's difficult to understand them. Regarding classes being interesting, it really has everything to do with your specific professor."

The College Prowler Take On...
Academics

During your first two years, you will most likely be busy taking required classes and won't actually meet a professor in your major until junior year. However, this is not to be seen as a drawback because even professors outside your major are generally knowledgeable in their field and always available for consultation or extra help. One thing is certain: Bentley professors do not want to see anyone fail and are willing to go out of their way so that it doesn't happen.

Because of the strong emphasis on a complete real-world business education, all of Bentley's professors may not actually be professors at all. There is a large percentage of instructors who are retired businesspeople who have already made their life's fortune and now use teaching as a way to supplement their lifestyle. The teaching styles vary from having only a traditional midterm and final exam to writing journal entries every night to offering extra credit for watching *The Apprentice*, but you can expect group work as a standard in any class.

The College Prowler® Grade on
Academics: B

A high Academics grade generally indicates that professors are knowledgeable, accessible, and genuinely interested in their students' welfare. Other determining factors include class size, how well professors communicate, and whether or not classes are engaging.

Local Atmosphere

The Lowdown On...
Local Atmosphere

Region:
Northeast

City, State:
Waltham, Massachusetts

Setting:
Small, metropolitan city

Distance from Boston:
15–20 minutes

Distance from Providence:
1 hour

Points of Interest:
Arnold Arboretum
Beacon Hill
Boston Public Library
Faneuil Hall
Fenway Park
Harvard Square (Cambridge)
Museum of Fine Arts
Newbury Street
Public Garden

Closest Shopping Malls or Plazas:

Burlington Mall

CambridgeSide Galleria

Natick Mall

Prudential Center Mall

Closest Movie Theaters:

AMC Burlington Cinema 10
20 South Ave.
(781) 229-9200

AMC Harvard Square
10 Church St., Cambridge
(617) 864-4580

Landmark Embassy Cinema
16 Pine St., Waltham
(781) 893-2500

Major Sports Teams:

Boston Bruins (hockey)

Boston Celtics (basketball)

Boston Red Sox (baseball)

New England Patriots (football)

City Web Sites

www.city.waltham.ma.us

www.discoverwaltham.com

www.waltham-community.org

www.walthamchamber.com

Did You Know?

5 Fun Facts about Waltham:

- **Boston's biggest hip hop radio station**, JAMN 94.5, is headquartered in Waltham.

- If you do your grocery shopping at Shaw's on Lexington Street in the winter, you may **bump into some celebrities**. Many Celtics players make their season home in Waltham.

- Check out ***www.walthamrocks.com***. No, it's not an ode to the city; rather, it's the Web site of an '80s rock cover band who paid the ultimate tribute to the city by naming themselves "Waltham."

- Waltham is called "**Watch City**" because the Waltham Watch Factory, founded in the 1850s, pioneered the mass production of watches.

- Waltham had one of the **first licenses to broadcast as a commercial TV station** in 1949, but the station was never built, and the license expired.

Famous People from Waltham:

F. Lee Bailey, famous attorney in the OJ Simpson trial

Local Slang:

(Local slang is not exclusive to Waltham; more appropriately, the local slang is used in the Boston area.)

Big Dig – Massive road construction project in Boston.

Bubbler – Water fountain.

Cool kid – Obnoxious, rude, and generally not wanted person.

Dunks – The coffee shop Dunkin' Donuts.

Frappe – A milkshake anywhere else; it's basically ice cream, milk, and chocolate syrup blended together.

Jimmies – Sprinkles.

Packy – A liquor store.

Students Speak Out On...
Local Atmosphere

"Waltham is a pretty large city. It's close to Boston and has good amount of bars and nightlife during the week. Brandeis is in Waltham, too, but we really do not interact too often. Boston's definitely a plus."

Q "Waltham is **a nice suburban town**. Brandeis University is also in town."

Q "Brandeis is here in Waltham, but **Boston is two seconds** away, so there are a million and one things to do all the time. It's also not a far drive to the beach, New Hampshire, Maine, or Rhode Island."

Q "There are a few other universities in the area. Many **clubs and bars around tend to be 18 and over**, which is great. It makes it somewhat easy to switch it up on the weekends, so you aren't always on campus. Waltham is an okay town. However, having Cambridge and Boston only a few minutes away puts Bentley College at a great location."

Q "Waltham is a nice town. **It is busy, but not too busy**. For those who crave craziness, Boston is right next door, where the possibilities are endless. There are many other colleges and universities in the area, so if you need a change, just visit Boston College, Northeastern, or Harvard."

Q "**Boston is great**, being that it is only a short shuttle or car ride away."

Q "**Bentley is very close** to Boston, so it is very convenient when you need to go out on the weekends or go shopping."

Q "There is **not much to do in the town**, but the free shuttle to Cambridge is convenient. Cambridge has good shopping and restaurants, and you can be in Boston in just a few minutes to get to clubs and other universities by taking the T."

Q "**Waltham is pretty boring**. There are so many universities around this town with Boston being only 10 miles away. With this in this mind, it's obvious there is plenty to do."

Q "**Waltham is kind of a sleepy town**, minus the restaurants. Brandeis is really close, though I never go there. I would recommend the restaurant Fire + Ice in Harvard Square, it's a little expensive, but the food is so good."

Q "**Waltham has a lot to offer**, but many students get stuck in what is called the 'Bentley bubble.' They do not extend their reach and make it a point to get away from the campus often enough, which I have noticed often results in students becoming burnt out of the Bentley scene by senior year."

Q "One word, 'suburbia.' At Bentley, you are only 10 miles or so away from Boston, but you feel like you are in the middle of nowhere due to its location in Waltham. From the period of January 19th until spring break, **I left campus a total of one time**. If you are without a car, the campus makes you feel very isolated."

Q "Waltham is small and doesn't have much to do, but obviously, **Boston is right there** with immense resources for fun!"

Q "**The atmosphere is good in Waltham** and great in Boston, but due to the lack of bars here in town, students are limited to parties on campus."

Q "**The school is great**, but the atmosphere is not that appealing because know one cares about Waltham. We're here to be at a business school, thus we all have similar thinking patterns."

Q "There is another college in Waltham, though **I never associate with Brandeis** and usually stay on campus. Frequently, I go into Boston on the free shuttle for fun."

Q "The town is great, but **there's not much to do here**. Even though Brandeis is in the same town, I have never met anyone that goes there."

Q "**Waltham is great**; it's close enough to Boston and Cambridge to make it an easy commute, and the shuttle makes it even easier. Brandeis is two miles away, so getting there for events is a piece of cake."

Q "Brandeis is also in Waltham, but I have never been there to hang out, and when **I go out locally**, I almost never run into Brandeis students. I don't think Waltham really has a college-town atmosphere, but Boston is just 10 minutes away."

The College Prowler Take On...
Local Atmosphere

If you were to take Bentley out of Waltham, the school dynamic wouldn't change that much, and the city wouldn't be upset for very long. There is a strange, yet often unspoken, love/hate relationship between Waltham and Bentley. Waltham loves to boast on its city Web sites how it has a rich academic tradition, yet it does little to nothing to encourage college students to want to become part of their community. Unlike other colleges in suburban cities, local Waltham businesses do not offer a student discount on things like food and school supplies to Bentley students. Many schools located directly in Boston have a partnership with restaurants that enable students to use their meal plan outside the college cafeteria; this is an unheard of concept here.

Bentley exists often in a world of its own. While students volunteer with local schools and homeless shelters, there isn't much for students to gain from the city of Waltham besides its proximity to Boston. It is the lack of a relationship that often overcomes students and keeps them from exploring the city. By the time senior year rolls around and most everyone is 21 and has a car on campus, it becomes obvious what a great culture and community Waltham has to offer. However, by that time, it is too late for anyone to form a bond with the city that they just lived in for four years, as they look to move back home or find a job in another nearby city. The major thing to remember about Waltham is that it is an up and coming Boston suburb, and it deserves a chance to be recognized for what it's worth.

B

The College Prowler® Grade on

Local
Atmosphere: B

A high Local Atmosphere grade indicates that the area surrounding campus is safe and scenic. Other factors include nearby attractions, proximity to other schools, and the town's attitude toward students

Safety & Security

The Lowdown On...
Safety & Security

Number of Bentley Police:

24

Bentley Police Phone:

(781) 891-3131
(emergencies)

(781) 891-2201
(non-emergencies)

Safety Services:

CPR and first-aid training

Dorm hall safety programs

Escort service

Rape aggression defense class
(RAD)

Student Health Services

175 Forest St.

(781) 891-2222

Services: Basic medical services, women's and men's health care, STD screening and treatment, lifestyle counseling, immunizations, health education

Health Center Office Hours

Monday 8 a.m.–5 p.m., Tuesday 8 a.m.–7 p.m., Wednesday 8 a.m.–5 p.m., Thursday 8 a.m.–5 p.m., Friday 8 a.m.– 4:30 p.m.

Students Speak Out On...
Safety & Security

"Security seems pretty tight here on campus. I have never felt threatened or unsafe when walking on campus alone at night."

Q "In my opinion, **security and safety on campus is great**. Never once have I felt that I wasn't safe or that my life was threatened."

Q "I feel both safe and secure on campus. **The campus police take care of things right away**, so there is no need to be nervous or scared while you are at Bentley."

Q "It's a very safe and secure campus. **I feel safe walking by myself** and at night."

Q "I always feel very safe on campus because **there is a large campus police force**, and you always see them driving around. The campus police are also friendly."

Q "I always feel safe here. I have no problem walking around at night, and I feel safe because **I see a cop drive by every time I am out on a walk**."

Q "This campus is very safe, but **it is not annoyingly strict** by any means. The Campus Police let us have our fun with barely any problems, but they are right there in case of emergency and handle serious matters extremely well."

Q "I feel very safe on campus, but I do not credit this to the Bentley Police Department. **I credit it to the judicial system here at Bentley** that does not tolerate fighting on campus at all."

Q "**It's pretty good, for the most part**. I do feel uncomfortable walking around on the weekend by myself late at night, but that is mostly due to the large abundance of male students and the peer pressures of getting intoxicated to the point of vomiting every weekend."

Q "**Campus Police sit in their cars all day**, and on the weekend they are on booze patrol."

Q "I never feel unsafe on campus. There is **a large campus security presence** and many cameras."

Q "Security is great on campus. **No complaints**! There are plenty of emergency phones in well-lit areas."

Q "**Security is minimal**; anyone can come on campus, and there is no dorm check-in."

Q "I feel fine, but **there are no cameras in parking lots** for cars. If your car gets hit while parked, Campus Police can't do anything about it."

Q "**Campus Police can be annoying**, especially with speeders and such, so if you are habitually late for class, living on campus is a must."

Q "I don't feel threatened whatsoever by the campus, and **there are plenty of those emergency call-boxes**."

The College Prowler Take On...
Safety & Security

If there is one negative aspect about the security on campus, it is the fact that no matter where you are on campus, you can't avoid running into Campus Police (CP). Most students understand that the strong police presence isn't necessarily a bad thing, and the joke is often, "Don't they have something better to do with their time?" The truth is, no, they don't. The campus is extremely safe, with the exception of the usual weekend stupid drunken incident, and students can walk around late at night without worry. CP doesn't take the safety for granted, though, and they offer various self-defense workshops for students and provide ongoing training to the officers.

Due to the lack of real crime on campus, it does leave the officers with a lot of free time. If you graduate without getting at least one parking violation from Campus Police, consider yourself blessed. Most students facetiously wish there was more for the officers to do because, on average, you will receive two parking violations in your four years here, and you can expect to pay around $150 in fines. The overall attitude towards Campus Police is negative, which is unfortunate, but students know that in the event of an emergency, CP will be there in record time ready to handle the situation, whether it's an incident of vandalism, a fight, or a fire alarm set off by burnt popcorn.

The College Prowler® Grade on

Safety & Security: B+

A high grade in Safety & Security means that students generally feel safe, campus police are visible, blue-light phones and escort services are readily available, and safety precautions are not overly necessary.

Computers

The Lowdown On...
Computers

High-Speed Network?
Yes

Wireless Network?
Yes

Number of Labs:
8

Number of Computers:
328

Operating Systems:
Mostly PCs; a few
Mac computers

Discounted Software

None available

Free Software

Software standard on Bentley-issued laptops include: Blackboard classroom, Connected Network Backup, Lotus Notes, Symantec AntiVirus, Windows XP

24-Hour Labs

None

Charge to Print?

No

Did You Know?

Every student is required to lease a laptop from Bentley, and it is upgraded to a newer version at the beginning of junior year. Upon graduation, you keep the laptop.

Bentley has collaborated with HP to allow students to work with their new Tablet PC to **conduct research on Tablet PC usage and acceptance**.

Bentley's Trading Room, an accounting and fianance lab with a ticker-tape display of real-time market data and constant financial news, was featured on CNBC. It was called **one of the top 10 trading room facilities in the country**, and is by far the largest.

Each classroom is wired with an Internet console for the professor and **Internet access at each desk for the students**.

Students Speak Out On...
Computers

"The most current up-to-date laptops are provided to all students and upgraded every two years. The network is extremely fast with little down time."

Q "**Bentley College provides students with computers** at a cost. They are great computers. I have yet to have a major problem with them. However, even if I did, the computer staff is very well trained and can handle any and all problems. The computer network is great."

Q "**At Bentley, you are required to buy the computer that they supply to you**; therefore, you don't have to worry about crowded labs. The networks are so quick, and surfing the Web is so easy."

Q "**The computer network here is amazing**. There are computer labs in the library as well as in Lindsay Hall near the computer resource center. Bringing your own computer is not necessary because Bentley issues a laptop to every student so that everyone is on the same computer playing field."

Q "Everyone has their own laptop, and sometimes we are required to bring them to class. The school's choice of laptops is good. **This year we have IBMs with CD burners and DVD-ROM drives**. The Internet connection is fast from the dorms, and the newer laptops also have wireless Internet access."

Q "**The computer network is unreal**, and the labs are plenty big. I recommend bringing your computer wherever you go."

Q "The computer situation is really good. Bentley makes everyone get the same laptop, which is definitely a plus because **everyone can help each other out**, and it's state-of-the-art technology. Internet connections are very vast, and wireless is becoming more available. Computer labs are used very sparingly—mostly if you have a ton of stuff to print out."

Q "**Since they give you a computer, bringing your own is not necessary**. The computer lab in the library is always busy, so it's best just to bring your own there. As for the network, I am very happy with Bentley's hard work to always remain connected."

Q "**The computer network is top-of-the-line**. If there is one thing that I like about Bentley it is the wired-ness of the campus. Visiting students need not bring a computer because there are many lounges around campus with network access."

Q "The computer **network is awesome**! Very high-tech with wireless Internet in all the newest laptops and Internet ports in almost every classroom. The classrooms are high-tech with video projectors, and so forth."

Q "Excellent computer network. **Computer labs are busy**, but there's always an extra seat. However, you will be given a laptop so it almost makes the computer lab unnecessary."

Q "**You don't need to bring your own computer**, as an overpriced one is provided for you. However, the network suffers quite a bit of downtime, and the computers are crap. Otherwise, not too bad though."

Q "**The labs are large**, and the network is one of the best in the country."

Q "The network rocks, but **no KaZaA or other music downloading is allowed**. Since every student has a laptop and each laptop works with the network, Internet access is excellent. I didn't bring my computer to campus, and I did just fine with the laptop; as a bonus, it's a DVD player and a CD burner, as well."

Q "One thing I can't really complain about at Bentley is the computer network. Though **the computer labs are sometimes kind of crowded**, the network speed here is probably unlike any other campus. It's a good thing I go to a school with lots of computer nerds!"

The College Prowler Take On...
Computers

Bentley's computer network is cutting-edge and very sophisticated. The state-of-the-art technology is visible no matter where you are on campus, which makes it hard to forget where all your tuition money goes. There is at least one computer in each classroom, yet many are equipped with computer consoles for each student. The laptop requirement is not forgotten in the classroom. In fact, there are power and network ports for each individual student's laptop in about half of the classrooms on campus. In the front of each classroom, there is a computer that is hooked up to a projector which allows for both professors and students to showcase educational material, pull up a Web site, or run a PowerPoint demonstration on a large screen in front of the class.

It's no wonder why Bentley is one of the most connected campuses in the country; the computer network runs off of a dual-T1 connection which allows for some of the fastest Internet connections around. Currently, there are a few wireless network "hotspots" around campus, mostly on upper campus, but the administration is continually trying to add more wireless connections. Within the network, there are many resources available to students. The "M: drive" is a resource that allows students to save files on a network drive that is accessible from any computer anywhere on campus as long as the student is logged in under their Bentley username and password. There is also the Bentley Virtual Lab, which allows students to access various programs that might be needed for use in a certain class. The use of Blackboard allows students and faculty to communicate and share class-related materials. One thing is for sure—every Bentley student, no matter what major, will graduate with an advanced knowledge of the latest computer software and networks that will place them above the rest of college graduates across the country.

A-

The College Prowler® Grade on
Computers: A-

A high grade in Computers designates that computer labs are available, the computer network is easily accessible, and the campus' computing technology is up-to-date.

Facilities

The Lowdown On...
Facilities

Student Center:
The Student Center and
LaCava Campus Center

Athletic Center:
The Charles A. Dana Center

Libraries:
Bentley College Library

Campus Size:
163 acres

Popular Places to Chill:
Coffeehouse
Student Center "ski lodge"
Smith study rooms

What Is There to Do on Campus?

Burn off some calories at the gym, grab some coffee at the Lower Café, hang out in the Backstage in the basement of Spruce Hall and shoot some pool, attend a networking event, or check out the latest edition of the *Vanguard*.

Movie Theater on Campus?

No, but every Sunday, CAB shows not-in-theater-but-not-yet-on-DVD movies in the Student Center.

Bowling on Campus?

No.

Bar on Campus?

Yes, the 1917 Tavern or "Pub" in the Student Center.

Coffeehouse on Campus?

Yes, Harry's Café in the bottom of Collins Hall, and the Lower Café in the LaCava Campus Center.

Favorite Things to Do

There is some type of activity offered almost every night of the week, whether it's a free movie, a comedy show, karaoke, or singers/songwriters in the Pub. Theme weeks are popular and bring new activities to campus such as arts and crafts nights, hot tubs on the Greenspace, and stress relief therapy. Intramural sports and club activities also keep students pretty busy.

Students Speak Out On...
Facilities

{ **"Everything is nice. The athletic center is older but they are keeping up with it, and rumor has it that there will be a new rec center in a few years with a new gym."**

Q "**Facilities here are really nice**. The Student Center is a new multi-million dollar building. Computers are new and up-to-date. The gym has many prime machines to work out on, as well as an indoor swimming pool that has open swim hours."

Q "The facilities on campus are great for the size of the school. **They are fairly new, always clean**, and respectable."

Q "**The Student Center is relatively new**. And all of the classrooms are run by computers, so with a touch, a computer screen turns the lights on or off and the window shades go down. The gym, swimming pool, and playing fields are all top of the line."

Q "The Student Center is only a few years old and very nice; however, **the athletic center needs some work**."

Q "Athletic facilities are nice, but **athletics overall are not really a main focus on the campus**. Although very successful, the administration does not put a lot of emphasis on them. Computers are good and up to date. The Student Center is new and up-to-date."

Q "I think all of **the buildings here are in good condition** compared to most schools."

Q "The facilities are nice. They're not junky, and they're not fit for a queen. I guess **they are just as nice as college facilities go**."

Q "**The technology on campus is wonderful**, and it keeps being updated. The facilities are generally nice, especially compared to other schools that I have seen."

Q "The facilities are excellent. **New dorms are constantly being built**, and the Dana Center is new, as well."

Q "All of the buildings, for the most part, are new and, for the most part, very clean. **The weight room needs some help**."

Q "The facilities all seem fairly new and in great condition. **Everything always feels clean**. Gardens are gorgeous—we have a fund set up by an alumnus which perpetually makes sure that the landscaping on Bentley campus is immaculate."

Q "Everything on campus is top-notch with **beautiful brick buildings and landscaping**."

Q "The facilities, for the most part, are new and up-to-date. I have found the weight room very advantageous; however, I can not say the same for other things. There are **racquetball courts being used for storage, and the basketball courts are rarely open**."

Q "Facilities are great on campus, but the gym could be renovated. **Computers are top-of-the-line**. The Student Center is brand new."

Q "**The gym is gross**. Smaller, less reputable schools have better gyms. The computers and Student Center are pretty nice."

The College Prowler Take On...
Facilities

The hub of student activity on campus can be found in the Student Center, located behind the Rhodes and Boylston apartments. Just over five years old, the Student Center quickly replaced the smaller, outdated former student center, LaCava, to become the mecca of anything related to student life. Still in its infancy, the Student Center has yet to be officially titled or given a proper nickname other than the highly unoriginal "Stu," which is mostly used by freshmen. With student organization offices on the third floor that overlook the Seasons Dining Hall on the second floor, there is an open, sunny feel to the building that makes it unique and unlike any other building on campus. Another exclusive feature is the study lounge, also dubbed the "Ski Lodge," on the second floor, characterized by high ceilings and a year-round working electric fireplace. The bottom floor is home to a large conference room that has been used for club dances and indoor activity fairs. The central location, welcoming design, and accessibility make the Student Center the most popular building on campus.

The administration has recognized how well the Student Center was received by students, and the Charles A. Dana Center has been a success as well—although many students complain about its inconvenient hours of operation. The number of non-athlete students using the gym facilities increases each year, and while new and extra equipment is added, the size of the space remains the same. Most academic buildings are beginning to show signs of aging with discolored wall paint and flooring tiles, but usually if there is a major problem, it will be fixed in a timely fashion. Due to student outcry, most dorms and suites have undergone, or are in the process of, major renovations to bring the rooms into the 21st century. With each building, both old and new, constructed mainly o brick, the campus has a uniform and professional look that never goes ou of style.

The College Prowler® Grade on

Facilities: B+

A high Facilities grade indicates that the campus is aesthetically pleasing and well-maintained; facilities are state-of-the-art, and libraries are exceptional. Other determining factors include the quality of both athletic and student centers and an abundance of things to do on campus.

Campus Dining

The Lowdown On...
Campus Dining

Freshman Meal Plan Requirement?
Yes

Meal Plan Average Cost:
$4,110–$4,850 annually

Places to Grab a Bite with Your Meal Plan:

Café a la Cart

Food: Starbucks, baked goods, fruit, salads, sandwiches, sides

Location: Adamian,1st floor

Hours: Monday–Thursday
8 a.m.–2 p.m.,
4:30 p.m.–9:30 p.m.,
Friday 8 a.m.–2 p.m.

Harry's Café

Food: Snacks, Good-to-Go prepared foods, subs, pizza, wraps, smoothies, bakery items, late-night pub fare

Location: Adamian, 1st floor

Hours: Monday–Thursday 8:15 a.m.–1 a.m.,
Friday 8:15 a.m.–2 a.m.,
Saturday 12 p.m.–2 a.m.,
Sunday 12 a.m.–1 a.m.

Lower Café

Food: Sushi, wraps, pizza, salad station, deli, grill

Location: LaCava Campus Center

Hours: Monday–Thursday 11 a.m.–7:30 p.m.,
Friday 11 a.m.–3 p.m.

Lower Café Express

Food: Starbucks coffee, smoothies, ice cream, bagels

Location: LaCava Campus Center

Hours: Monday–Thursday 7:30 a.m.–7:30 p.m.,
Friday 7:30 a.m.–3 p.m.

Seasons Dining Hall

Food: Pizza, grill, stir-fry, hot entrees, wraps, vegetarian, soup, salad bar, deli bar, desserts, frozen yogurt, ice cream, waffles

Location: Student Center

Hours: Monday–Thursday 7:30 a.m.–9 p.m.,
Friday 7:30 a.m.–8 p.m.,
Saturday 11 a.m.–8 p.m.,
Sunday 11 a.m.–9 p.m.

Off-Campus Places to Use Your Meal Plan:

None

24-Hour On-Campus Eating?

No

Student Favorites:

Harry's Café

Seasons Dining Hall

Did You Know?

If you are unhappy with the dining services, **drop a comment to the cafeteria manger**. Not only does a manager respond to your comment quickly, but they will post the comment and plan of action for all students to see.

Other Options

Several years ago, the "Sub Man," the popular late-night snack fix for students, was kicked off campus for not having proper permits to sell subs from the back of his car. It will be a wonderful thing for all when and if the mysterious Sub Man returns.

Students Speak Out On...
Campus Dining

> "Seasons is the main dining hall on campus where an unlimited meal plan is offered. The food is good, but it gets repetitive very quickly. Lower Café is great when you need a change. The food is excellent there, and the atmosphere is relaxed and fun."

Q "Food is okay. A **good amount of variety**, but not always the best quality. Compared to other schools I have eaten at, though, Bentley is so much better."

Q "Food on campus is **nothing special**. It gets old very soon. Restaurants in the surrounding area, however, are worth a look at."

Q "**The food on campus is not too bad**. The best place to eat is the Lower Café."

Q "**Food is improving constantly**, and the late-night deli/convenience store is great to have."

Q "The quality of the food in the cafeteria changes a lot. The pizza and grilled chicken are usually good, but **there could be more options for vegetarians** and a better salad bar. The Café, which is only open for lunch, has good sushi and designer salads."

Q "Dinning hall is nice. Food could use a lot more variety. **Lower Café is a lot better**, but the food takes a lot longer to cook."

Q "**Campus food is cafeteria food**. I have eaten at better schools, but I have also eaten at worse."

Q "I don't mind the food on campus. All of the fattening food is very good, and some of the healthier stuff is good, as well, and **there's always a Panera down the street** if you get sick of it."

Q "The food is good when you have a very limited meal plan, but if you have the **unlimited meal plan** and that is where you get all of your meals, then it begins to get repetitious."

Q "There is **a lack of options**; the only places you can go to eat are the main dining hall, which prepares low-quality food for the hefty price of the meal plan, and the Lower Café, which generally has the same offering as the main cafeteria (wraps, grill items, pizza)."

Q "Food is boring after a little while. **Good at first**, but then the variety turns into different variations of the same thing—pretty much all junk food and very little healthy food, so our discretionary money has to be used on crap food."

Q "Food is decent, but **the required meal plan is a freaking rip off**."

Q "Food is pretty good. **Dining Services listen to your suggestions and make changes**. The only real cafeteria is Seasons. There are a few other stands and small delis.

Q "The LaCava cafeteria is excellent, providing sushi, Starbucks, and steak and cheese for eating between classes. The Seasons Dining Hall near the dorms is very complete, with a little bit of everything. The **food could be better**, but if you have ever eaten at, say, UMass, or even Brandeis, you know that it could be a heck of a lot worse, too."

Q "The food is terrible, and **the meal plan must be one of the most expensive in the country**. Most students are forced to be on the unlimited meal plan with housing through a greedy agreement Bentley has with Sodexho."

The College Prowler Take On...
Campus Dining

For food on campus, the main option is Seasons Dining Hall. Even though students love to complain about on-campus food, the truth is that the cafeteria is not really all that bad. Compared to other local college cuisine, Bentley has it pretty darn good. Sodexho, the company in charge of all campus eateries, is constantly changing meal plan options based on student feedback surveys. Recent additions to the Seasons dining room include a wrap station and increased vegetarian options desired by students. Harry's Café is always busy just before a class period begins and during late-night hours when students need the extra caffeine kick to finish pumping out the papers.

The one complaint about on-campus dining that cannot be ignored is the hefty price the required meal plan carries. While the food is good, it's not that good. Typically, the meal plan has a "discretionary" component where you can buy coffee or a sandwich in the deli, and Sodexho has been playing around with the percentage of discretionary versus number of times the meal plan is valid in a week. It's easy to forget the value of a dollar when using the discretionary money because it's not actual money out of your pocket, but as soon as you use that money up, you will find it really hard to pay $6 for a pint of Ben & Jerry's in the ridiculously overpriced deli. One of the biggest joys of getting out of dorm life is the opportunity to opt out of a meal plan and begin buying and cooking food on your own; that is until you realize what a pain dishes can be.

The College Prowler® Grade on

Campus Dining: C+

Our grade on Campus Dining addresses the quality of both school-owned dining halls and independent on-campus restaurants as well as the price, availability, and variety of food.

Off-Campus Dining

The Lowdown On...
Off-Campus Dining

Restaurant Prowler:
Popular Places to Eat!

Absolutely Asia
Food: Chinese
864 Main St., Waltham
(781) 891-1700
www.absolutelyasia.com
Price: $6–$15 per person
Hours: Sunday–Thursday
11 a.m.–10 p.m., Friday–
Saturday 11a.m.–12 a.m.

Angelo's House of Pizza
Food: Pizza, subs
579 Moody St., Waltham
(781) 893-1208
Price: $5–$13 per person
Hours: Sunday–Thursday
11 a.m.–10 p.m., Friday–
Saturday 11 a.m.–11 p.m.

BaanThai
Food: Thai, sushi
657 Main St., Waltham
(781) 893-7700
www.baanthaifood.com

(Baan Thai, continued)

Cool Features: Waiters dress in traditional Thai clothing.

Price: $7–$15 per person

Hours: Monday–Saturday, 11:30 a.m.–3 p.m., 5 p.m.–10 p.m., Sunday 5 p.m.–10 p.m.

Bison County

Food: Texas/Southern style barbeque

275 Moody St., Waltham

(781) 642-9720

www.bisoncounty.com

Cool Features: Serves bison burgers!

Price: $6–$25 per person

Hours: Monday–Thursday 11:30 p.m.–10:30 a.m., Friday–Saturday 12 a.m.–11:30 a.m.

Border Café

32 Church St., Cambridge

(617) 864-6100

Price: $6–$14 per person

Hours: Monday–Thursday 10 a.m.–12:45 a.m., Friday–Saturday, 11 a.m.–1:45 a.m., Sunday 12 p.m.–12:45 a.m.

Chateau Restaurant

Food: Italian

195 School St., Waltham

(781) 894-3339

www.chateaurestaurant.com

Price: $12–$22 per person

Hours: Sunday–Wednesday 11:15 a.m.–9 p.m., Thursday

(Chateau Restaurant, continued)

11:15 a.m.–10 p.m., Friday–Saturday 11:15 a.m.–10:30 p.m.

Fire + Ice

50 Church St., Cambridge

(617) 547-9007

http://fire-ice.com

Price: $8–$16 per person

Special features: Create-your-own stir-fry.

Hours: Monday–Thursday 11:30 a.m.–10 p.m., Friday–Saturday 11:30 a.m.–11 p.m., Sunday 10 a.m.–3 p.m.

John Brewer's Tavern

Food: American

39 Main St., Waltham

(781) 894-9700

www.johnbrewerstavern.com

Price: $9–$15 per person

Hours: Monday–Saturday 11:30 a.m.–11 p.m., Sunday 12 p.m.–10:45 p.m.

Margaritas

Food: Mexican

227 Moody St., Waltham

(781) 893-9990

Cool Features: Outdoor eating on the Charles River; huge party every full moon.

Price: $10–$15 per person

Hours: Sunday–Thursday 4 p.m.–10 p.m., Friday–Saturday 4 p.m.–11 p.m.

New York Deli Pizzeria

Food: Sandwiches, wraps, salads, pizza

47 Lexington St., Waltham

(781) 894-1228

www.newyorkdelipizzeria.com

Price: $6–$10 per person

Hours: Daily 10 a.m.–11 p.m.

Not Your Average Joe's

Food: Italian, American, Asian

55 Main St., Watertown

(617) 926-9229

www.notyouraveragejoes.com

Price: $3–$20 per person

Hours: Monday–Thursday 11:30 a.m.–10 p.m., Friday–Saturday 11:30 a.m.–11 p.m., Sunday 12 a.m.–10 p.m.

Panera Bread

Food: Sandwiches, salads, soup, bagels, pastries

1100 Lexington St., or 395 Arsenal St., Watertown

Lexington: (781) 547-5655

Arsenal: (617) 923-2918

www.panera.com

Price: $6–$10 per person

Hours: Lexington: Monday–Thursday 6 a.m.–9 p.m., Friday 6 a.m.–10 p.m., Saturday 7 a.m.–10 p.m., Sunday 7 a.m.–9 p.m.

Arsenal: Monday–Saturday 6 a.m.–9 p.m., Sunday 6 a.m.–8 p.m.

So-Cal Restaurant

Food: Wraps, salads, vegetarian

484 Moody St., Waltham

(781) 647-8090

www.socalrestaurant.com

Price: $10 per person

Hours: Monday–Friday 10 a.m.–9:30 p.m., Saturday 10 a.m.–9 p.m., Sunday 11 a.m.–9 p.m.

Solea Restaurant & Tapas Bar

Food: Spanish, South American

388 Moody St., Waltham

(781) 894-1805

www.solearestaurant.com

Cool Features: Large windows in front that open in spring and summer months.

Price: $20–$24 per person, or $6–$15 for tapas

Hours: Monday–Wednesday 5 p.m.–10 p.m., Thursday–Saturday 12 p.m.–11 p.m. Sunday 12 p.m.–10 p.m.

Watch City Brewing Co.

Food: American, microbrew pub

256 Moody St., Waltham

(781) 647-4000

www.watchcitybrew.com

Price: $8–$20 and under

Hours: Monday–Saturday 11:30 a.m.–10 p.m., Friday–Saturday 11:30 a.m.–10:30 p.m., Sunday 4 p.m.–9 p.m.

Wendy's
806 Main St., Waltham
(781) 899-2795
www.wendys.com
Cool Features: Dollar menu.
Hours: Sunday–Wednesday
10 a.m.–11 p.m. (drive-thru
until 1 a.m.), Thursday–
Saturday 10 a.m.–12 a.m.
(drive-thru open until 2 a.m.)

Wilson's Diner
Food: American, breakfast
507 Main St., Waltham
(781) 899-0760
Price: $4–$10 per person
Hours: Monday–Friday
5:15 a.m.–3 p.m., Saturday–
Sunday 6:15 a.m.–2 p.m.

Other Places to Check Out:

Asian Grill

Bertucci's Brick Oven Pizzeria

Bombay Club

Boston Market

Burger King

Carl's Steak Subs

Casa Mia

Iguana Cantina

Joe Sent Me

Lizzy's Ice Cream Parlor

Naked Fish

Pete's Pizza & Wings

Sal's Ristorante & Pizzeria

Shilla Restaurant

Skellig Irish Music Pub

Uno Chicago Pizza

Student Favorites:
Margaritas
Panera Bread
So-Cal Restaurant
Wilson's Diner

Late-Night Eating:
Wendy's

Closest Grocery Stores:
Shaw's
130 River St., Waltham
(781) 647-5341

Star Market
1070 Lexington St., Waltham
(781) 891-0615

Super Stop & Shop
700 Pleasant St., Watertown
(617) 923-3007

Best Pizza:
Angelo's House of Pizza

Best Chinese:
Absolutely Asia

Best Breakfast:
Wilson's Diner

Best Wings:
Bison County

Best Healthy:
So-Cal Restaurant

**Best Place to Take
Your Parents:**
Not Your Average Joe's
Solea Restaurant & Tapas Bar
Watch City Brewing Co.

Students Speak Out On...
Off-Campus Dining

{ **"Students in the dorms are inundated with take-out menus for Chinese, Italian, and wings. The food is decent but not great, though it's sometimes a nice change from the cafeteria."**

Q "There are **a lot of nice restaurants in Harvard Square**. Bombay Club is good for Indian food, and Border Café is good for Mexican food. There is also a Bertucci's and Pizzeria Uno. Panera Bread is a great place for a quick lunch in Waltham."

Q "Tons of good places. **Lizzy's Ice Cream, Iguana Cantina and Margaritas** are all on Moody St., which has tons of bars and restaurants. There are tons of places that deliver, and there's tons of food in Harvard Square and Boston."

Q "There are many restaurants that deliver right to your door. Some other fun spots, when you want to get out of your room, like **Fire + Ice and Border Café, are in Harvard Square, which is only a shuttle ride away**."

Q "**A lot of restaurants around Waltham are within 10 minutes from campus**. In Waltham, Casa Mia is a really nice Italian restaurant on Newton Street. Chateau is good, too, on School Street."

Q "I don't really eat off campus very often, but there is a great little Japanese and Korean place called **Shilla in Harvard Square**."

Q "**I personally like Panera Bread** because is it relatively healthy and inexpensive."

Q "There are many good restaurants off campus on Moody Street and around that area, but many **students don't get off campus enough** to go experience them."

Q "If you are interested in going to a restaurant off campus, **your main options are located in Harvard Square**. Waltham has an abundance of takeout restaurants, which is excellent because I would rate the campus food subpar."

Q "Tons of good places to eat in Harvard square. In Waltham, **Panera Bread or New York Deli are good** for lunch."

Q "You can get any type of food you want. **Margaritas has good Mexican**. John Brewer's for 10 cent wings. New York Deli for subs. Pete's Wings for, well, wings."

Q "There is generally **good food available off-campus**. Carl's Steaks off of Main Street has the best steak subs anywhere in the Boston area."

Q "I haven't really been to any restaurants off campus except for Boston Market once. I know **there is a Burger King and Wendy's really close by**."

Q "There is **a great wide range from expensive to cheap**. Expensive options would be Naked Fish and Fire + Ice, while the cheap route is Sal's."

Q "**Asian Grill is reasonably priced** and delicious with good portions."

The College Prowler Take On...
Off-Campus Dining

Students don't get off campus enough to enjoy the plethora of quality restaurants in Waltham. Students are drawn to the dining experience in Harvard Square due to the allure and ease of the free college shuttle, but in reality, Waltham has double the amount of restaurant options. The diversion away from Waltham establishments starts young, since freshmen are not allowed to have cars on campus, thus making the shuttle to Harvard very appealing. By the time you are allowed to have a car on campus, you will find yourself stuck in the routine of continuing to go into Harvard Square to eat out and won't explore your local community.

The highlight of off-campus dining is Moody Street, which boasts the Bentley favorite, Margaritas, along with the staple pub food at the Skellig and Joe Sent Me. Moody Street, four years ago, had a very different look and feel than it does now, but that has yet to have an effect on student dining patterns. However, with virtually every ethnic cuisine represented, it would be hard not to find something enticing. The local shuttle service is now defunct, but a taxi from Bentley to Main and Moody would be a few bucks and well worth it for a gourmet meal in your backyard.

The College Prowler® Grade on

Off-Campus
Dining: B+

A high off-campus dining grade implies that off-campus restaurants are affordable, accessible, and worth visiting. Other factors include the variety of cuisine and the availability of alternative options (vegetarian, vegan, Kosher, etc.).

Campus Housing

The Lowdown On...
Campus Housing

Undergrads Living On Campus:
80%

Best Dorms:
Boylstons
Copleys
Fenway

Worst Dorms:
Rhodes
Trees

Number of Dorms:
11

Number of University-Owned Apartments and Houses:
7

→

Dormitories:

Boylston A & B Apartments

Floors: 5

Total Occupancy: 140; Boylston A (70), Boylston B (70)

Bathrooms: In-room

Coed: Yes

Residents: Upperclassmen

Room Types: 4-person apartments, 2- and 3-person suites

Special Features: Laundry, lounge

Cape House

Floors: 3

Total Occupancy: 10

Bathrooms: Shared by floor

Coed: Yes

Residents: Upperclassmen

Room Types: One 2-person apartment, one 5-person apartment, one 4-person apartment

Special Features: Laundry, kitchen, lounge

Castle House

Floors: 2

Total Occupancy: 7

Bathrooms: Shared by floor

Coed: Yes

Residents: Upperclassmen

Room Types: Traditional single

Special Features: Lounge, kitchen

Collins Hall

Floors: 7

Total Occupancy: 256

Bathrooms: In-room

Coed: Yes

Residents: Upperclassmen

Room Types: 2- and 4-person apartments, single apartments

Special Features: Function room, Fleet ATM, study room, weight room, laundry

Copley Suites

Floors: 4

Total Occupancy: 319; Copley North (164), Copley South (155)

Bathrooms: In-room

Coed: Yes

Residents: Juniors and seniors

Room Types: 2-, 3-, 4-, and 6-person suites

Special Features: Laundry, living room, game room, study room on each floor, common bathrooms on ground floor

Falcone Apartments

Floors: 3

Total Occupancy: 212; Falcone East (65), Falcone North (82), Falcone West (65)

Bathrooms: In-room

Coed: Yes

Residents: Upperclassmen

Room Types: 2- and 5-person apartments

Special Features: Function room, kitchen, exercise room, study room, TV lounge, laundry

Fenway Hall

Floors: 4

Total Occupancy: 286

Bathrooms: In-room

Coed: Yes

Residents: Juniors and seniors

Room Types: 4- and 6-person suites

Special Features: Laundry, living room, game room, function room, kitchen, study room on each floor

Forest Suites

Floors: 5

Total Occupancy: 276

Bathrooms: In-room

Coed: Yes

Residents: Mostly sophomores

Room Types: 6-, 7-, or 8-person suites

Special Features: Study lounge, laundry, recreation room, common bathrooms on ground floor, function room

Kresge Hall

Floors: 5

Total Occupancy: 233

Bathrooms: In-room

Coed: Yes

Residents: Sophomores and juniors

Room Types: 4- and 5-person suites

Special Features: Laundry, study lounge, recreation room

Miller Hall

Floors: 4

Total Occupancy: 244

Bathrooms: Shared by floor

Coed: Yes

Residents: Mostly freshmen, some sophomores

Room Types: Traditional small single, large single, double, triple, quad

Special Features: Social/TV lounge, kitchen, laundry

Nathan R. Miller Hall

Floors: 4 plus basement

Total Occupancy: 244

Bathrooms: In-room

Coed: Yes

Residents: Mostly freshmen, some upperclassmen

Room Types: Small singles, large singles, doubles, triples, quads

Special Features: Mail room, large social/TV lounge, kitchen, laundry room, vending

North Campus Apartments

Floors: 2 two-story complexes

Total Occupancy: 116

Bathrooms: Private

Coed: Yes

Residents: Grad students

Room Types: 2-, 3-, and 4-person apartments

Special Features: Laundry, study lounge, barbeque pits, bike racks, ample parking

Orchard (North and South) Apartments

Floors: 4

Total Occupancy: 195; North (60), South (135)

Bathrooms: In-room

Residents: Upperclassmen

Room Types: 5-person apartments

Special Features: Laundry (North and South), study lounges on each floor, function room/kitchen (North), parking in the new parking deck behind Orchard North

Rhodes Hall

Floors: 4

Total Occupancy: 160

Bathrooms: In-room

Coed: Yes

Residents: Upperclassmen

Room Types: 2- and 4-person apartments

Special Features: Laundry, Student Health Services (ground floor)

Slade Hall

Floors: 4

Total Occupancy: 239

Bathrooms: Shared by floor

Coed: Yes

Residents: Mostly freshmen, some sophomores

Room Types: Traditional small single room, large single room, double room, triple room, quad room

(Slade Hall, continued)

Special Features: Study lounges, social/ TV lounge, laundry, two racquetball courts, universal weight-lifting machines, kitchen/function room

Stratton House

Floors: 3

Total Occupancy: 10

Bathrooms: Shared by floor

Coed: Yes

Residents: Upperclassmen

Room Types: Traditional single

Special Features: Kitchen, lounge, laundry, study, deck off the back of the house, separate from rest of residence halls

Trees Complex (network of 7 traditional residence halls)

Floors: 4

Total Occupancy: 480; Alder Hall (83), Birch Hall (67), Cedar Hall (67), Elm Hall (63), Maple Hall (66), Oak Hall (58), Spruce Hall (76)

Bathrooms: Shared by floor

Coed: Yes

Residents: Freshmen

Room Types: Traditional double and triple rooms

Special Features: TV Lounge/ kitchen (Maple Hall), study lounges (ground floors of Cedar and Oak Halls), laundry (Elm Hall), backstage lounge (Spruce Hall)

Housing Offered:

Singles: 10%

Doubles: 57%

Triples/Suites: 2%

Apartments: 31%

Room Types

Residence rooms include traditional, suite, and apartment units.

Traditional – Students share a large, central bathroom facility (all first-year students are assigned to these rooms).

Suite – Students share a private bathroom and common living area with no more than seven students. Rooms are equipped with a sink and MicroFridge unit.

Apartment – Students share a private bathroom, common living area, and in-room kitchen with no more than four students.

Houses are on campus and typically for those with special housing needs.

Bed Type

Twin extra-long (39"x 80"); bunk beds in small double rooms

Cleaning Service?

Shared and public bathrooms are cleaned by staff daily. Suites and apartments are not cleaned.

What You Get

Bed, desk, chair, closet, dresser, window coverings, cable TV jack, Ethernet, free campus and local phone calls. Suites and apartments also get a coffee table, couch, chairs, and various tables.

Did You Know?

All buildings are **smoke-free**.

All campus residents get **free cable** and access to Bentley's movie channel.

Living in Collins Hall or the Orchard Apartments means you agree to have **other students living in your room** during winter break.

Students Speak Out On...
Campus Housing

"Dorms here are good. My friends who come to visit remark on how big my room is. Slade and Miller are the best freshman dorms to get."

"**The dorms are good**; air-conditioning and heat that you control, clean carpets, and bathrooms are cleaned every day. No building is bad, some are louder then others, but you can pick where you want to be after your first year."

"The dorms are nice. As a freshman, I got lucky and ended up staying in Miller. **The Trees are the real freshman dorm**, and I wouldn't recommend it; it is very similar to a maze. All of the upperclassman dorms are real nice, especially those on lower campus, but that means a long walk to classes. The newest dorm, Fenway, should be real nice."

"**New dorms are always built**, and after freshman year, suites and apartments are most common to get."

"All the dorms, in general, are nice. **The apartment-style dorms are the coolest** and most sought-after, and they do not require the meal plan fee."

"Dorms overall are good. **Freshman dorms are obviously pretty small** compared to others. The newer dorms are really nice and good-sized."

Q "The dorms here are pretty nice. **They are all very well kept**. Since they are building new ones all over the place, things are looking better. Avoid any of the Trees. And try for Miller your freshman year. Other than that, go for the new ones such as Copley or Fenway, and then senior year, go for the Falcone apartments."

Q "The dorms are okay. **Avoid the Trees**; the rooms are small, and it's far away from everything. But the up-side to it is that there are a lot of people in the Trees, probably most of the freshman class. After freshman year, most everyone gets a suite or an apartment-style dorm."

Q "All the dorms are nice, but **the best ones are the newest ones down on Lower Campus** (Copley and Fenway). The nice one on Upper Campus is Falcone, but the party building is Collins, for sure."

Q "I would **avoid the Orchard dorms and Rhodes**. Nothing ever happens in Rhodes—it has small rooms that are always quiet with nothing going on."

Q "The freshman housing at Bentley consists of **small rooms that are either doubles, triples, or quads**. They aren't great, but they aren't terrible; they are typical dormitory-style rooms. For upperclassmen, there are suites and apartments—suites not having full kitchens as opposed to apartments that do. Those are all generally nice; the ones on South Campus are newer, which is the only big difference."

Q "**Slade is the place to be for incoming freshman students**. It's newer, and it's been repainted and carpeted recently. The Trees are smaller in room size, much older, and need redecorating. Miller is the other option for freshman housing, but it is far away from all the other freshmen, and a lot of upperclassmen house there, too."

Q "**The dorms, overall, are all very well maintained**. The new suites are about the best (Copley North, Copley South, and Fenway) and similar to a nice hotel."

Q "**The dorms are great; upperclassman apartments are unreal**, and the freshman dorms are great as far as freshman dorms go."

Q "The dorms are okay. The good ones are the apartments in Falcone, Collins, Boylston, and Orchard. There is also **a new, huge dorm that is very nice** (tall windows, big rooms, and a nice view) called Fenway."

Q "The dorms aren't bad. We have beautiful new dorms on Lower Campus, but that's usually reserved for second-year housing. **There really aren't apartments and houses next to campus**, so most students end up staying in on-campus housing for the four years."

Q "**The dorms are good overall**, apart from the ridiculous meal plan requirement in most buildings. Falcone Apartments are the best, while the newer Fenway suites and recently-built Copley Suites are hotel-like."

The College Prowler Take On...
Campus Housing

After the mandatory struggle of living in the freshman dorms, life will get much sweeter sophomore year as you make the choice between one of the three new suites on lower campus. Junior and senior year give independent living a new meaning as you begin your stay in an on-campus apartment. The major change happens after your tenure in the Trees, Miller, or Slade when you move into one of the Copleys or Fenway. After sharing a bathroom with 20 other people, having your own personal bathroom inside your suite is well worth the hassle of cleaning it yourself. The in-room fridge and microwave are a great transition into apartment living and an assurance that you won't starve if the cafè doesn't have anything appetizing. While most students live on campus all four years, it's because they choose to, not simply because of the lack of off-campus options. The housing options are almost as top-notch as the computer network, with a style of room to fit anyone's tastes and needs. The furniture could be newer, and the rugs should be cleaned more frequently, but overall, the dorm rooms, suites, and apartments are comfortable and easy to live in.

The small-school feel of Bentley can be alienating to someone living off campus because on-campus housing is where friends and bonds are made, often at late-night study sessions or hanging out in the student lounge. The actual facilities are all new and up-to-date or, at least, renovated to look that way.

B+

The College Prowler® Grade on
Campus Housing:
B+

A high Campus Housing grade indicates that dorms are clean, well-maintained, and spacious. Other determining factors include variety of dorms, proximity to classes, and social atmosphere.

Off-Campus Housing

The Lowdown On...
Off-Campus Housing

Undergrads Living Off Campus:

20%

Average Rent for:

Studio Apt.: $950/month

1BR Apt.: $1,100/month

2BR Apt.: $1,300/month

Popular Areas:

Brighton/Allston

Moody Street

Windsor Village

Best Time to Look for a Place:

July or August

Students Speak Out On...
Off-Campus Housing

"It's better to stay on campus; you miss a lot if you move off campus. It's also much more expensive to live off because housing in Boston is so costly."

"**Living off campus is not worth it** because housing is guaranteed all four years, and living on campus means you are so close to everything going on, from your classes to everyday campus life."

"**You might save some money living off campus** because you won't have the meal plan, but you really need a car if you want to do that."

"I have heard that living off campus is nice, but most people enjoy living here. **People stay here on the weekends, so it's fun**."

"Housing off campus is not worth it because **the people who live off campus become out of touch** with the people who live on campus."

"**Bentley no longer offers off-campus housing**. You used to be able to get housing through the Windsor Village (two minutes away), but the college no longer sponsors that. Now students have to go through Windsor directly, but I still feel this is a better deal than living on campus because it is cheaper, and you don't have to deal with all the rules the college enforces."

Q "**Living off campus is fairly convenient**. It's worth it financially if you have a car, but you will miss out on a social life."

Q "I don't think it's worth it; living off campus seems too out of the way and **makes people anti-social from campus**, but I haven't personally tried it."

Q "Off-campus housing is very convenient; it is a bit pricey, but **you can find all the space you need** if you have the money to spend."

Q "You can get it; however, **it is more convenient and sometimes nicer to just live on campus**."

Q "**Housing off campus varies** with how many people you are going to be living with; if you can find three to four other people, you can easily rent an awesome house for less per person than on-campus housing."

The College Prowler Take On...
Off-Campus Housing

The choice to live off campus is not very popular; however, finding nearby accommodations is fairly easy. Bentley does not offer apartment search assistance, but this is not a problem, as there are plenty of options that students use year after year. The Windsor Apartments probably have the highest percentage of students living off campus in one area, and since they were once affiliated with Bentley, students find their rates reasonable and their location very convenient. Living in a Waltham apartment can enable you to still feel connected to the Bentley nightlife and social scene; however, living anywhere beyond Waltham automatically makes you a commuter student. There is little to no interaction between commuters and on-campus residents.

Many transfer and international students make their home in the Allston/Brighton area because of the close proximity to bars and nightclubs. The closer to the city you get, the more expensive the rent, and it becomes necessary to either be financially stable or have multiple roommates to split the costs. The best kept secret in finding an off-campus apartment is to check out *http://boston.craigslist.org* for sublets, roommate searches, and to find the abode of your off-campus dreams.

The College Prowler® Grade on

Off-Campus Housing: C

A high grade in Off-Campus Housing indicates that apartments are of high quality, close to campus, affordable, and easy to secure.

Diversity

The Lowdown On...
Diversity

American Indian:
Less than 1%

White:
77%

Asian American:
7%

International:
8%

African American:
4%

Out-of-State:
45%

Hispanic:
4%

Political Activity

Being a business school, most students are fairly conservative, and those with more liberal ideas do not feel as comfortable sharing their opinions. The Young Republicans Club has a strong presence on campus and often brings controversial speakers to campus.

Gay Pride

PRIDE, Bentley's gay, lesbian, and transgendered club, is one of the best-known, yet underappreciated, organizations on campus. There is a shift happening right now at Bentley towards increasing acceptance and tolerance of all minority groups, and it is starting with the gay community. An active student who is "out" on campus usually advocates education and understanding to those unfamiliar with what it's like being gay.

Most Popular Religions

There are a variety of active Christian groups. A "Sacred Space" was created in the new student center for all religions to share. After 9/11, there is a stronger feeling of spirituality on campus.

Economic Status

You may not see it at first, but the majority of students here come from money. Designer clothes and the attitudes to go with them are far too common. If you don't have the money to buy Gucci or Prada, you aren't necessarily looked down upon, but once you realize the economic divide that exists here, it's hard to ignore.

Minority Clubs

Behind the Campus Activities Board, NABA (National Association of Black Accountants) is the largest club on campus. African American students in NABA are highly respected and a vocal force. NABA and several Asian clubs often put on parties and events to encourage new members to join.

Students Speak Out On...
Diversity

> **"There are some minorities and a lot of international students, but you don't see a lot of people who come from low-income backgrounds."**

Q "I find this campus to be **pretty diverse**, especially compared to my high school."

Q "**The campus is incredibly diverse**. That is one of the best things about it. It is great to meet lots of different people, and Bentley allows you to."

Q "**The student population is predominantly white** and from the New England area, but there are also many international students."

Q "Not extremely diversified among students from the U.S.; however, **there is a lot of diversity in terms of international kids**."

Q "**Minorities are definitely represented**. However, as far as mingling with other races goes, well, it just doesn't happen. It's very frustrating because everyone judges everyone else."

Q "It's pretty diverse, but it's also **a pretty small campus**."

Q "This campus is relatively diverse. You will end up with several international friends, whether you like it or not. About **17 percent of the students are international**, and they are all very interesting."

Q "There are many international students here on campus, but **they tend to exclude themselves by living off campus with each other**. They don't put much effort into getting to know people who live here on campus."

Q "The campus is diverse, but **the school does little to facilitate interaction between ethnic groups**. They sponsor events mainly for international students and students with different ethnic backgrounds to meet each other, not white students."

Q "Very diverse in population, but the only problem is that all **the ethnic groups only hang out within themselves**. There is very little mixing of races among social groups, which seems like it defeats the purpose of diversity to me!"

Q "Campus is **somewhat diverse**, but still mostly white."

Q "**There are lot of international students**, but also a lot of people from New England and New York area."

Q "Not diverse enough. There seem to be **a lot of African men, but not black American men**."

Q "Not very diverse. The white-hat crowd is predominant, with **lots of jock/frat types**."

Q "**Lots of foreigners**: the Latin American population is pretty big, along with the Middle Eastern and Indian populations. The African American population isn't too big, but to tell you the truth, they all seem to stick together. I always see a group of like 20–30 African American students at the caf together."

The College Prowler Take On...
Diversity

The issue of diversity on campus is divided amongst those who see it and those who don't. Mostly, students agree that it is more diverse than their high schools, but not as diverse as other local colleges. If you're from the U.S., you are most likely very similar to everyone else on campus that is from the U.S. However, the international student population is very diverse; over 50 countries are represented. Usually, any non-American student is lumped into the "international" category, whether they are from Brazil, Germany, or Japan. In order to make friends with someone from a different country, culture, or background than you, it really has to become a personal initiative to break the barrier that exists between American and non-American students.

As a business school, it is important for Bentley to advertise the diverse student population, enticing prospective students to experience the rich culture of another country, but there is hardly any follow-through on that promise beyond first year studies. With the exception of a few freshman courses and any international business course, the topic of diversity is rarely touched upon in the classroom. It is easy to see the different types of students in any given course, and at times, international students will be asked about the business environment in their home country. The situation outside the class is another story, and the interaction between international and U.S.-born students is forced and unnatural.

The College Prowler® Grade on

Diversity: C+

A high grade in Diversity indicates that ethnic minorities and international students have a notable presence on campus and that students of different economic backgrounds, religious beliefs, and sexual preferences are well-represented.

Guys & Girls

The Lowdown On...
Guys & Girls

Men Undergrads:	**Women Undergrads:**
41%	59%

Birth Control Available?

Condoms are available in health services for free. Female students can have an exam at health services, but they need to have their prescription filled at a local pharmacy. Sometimes, if it is the first time a female is going on birth control, the nurse will give you a free pack of pills.

Social Scene

Get ready for high school all over again. The amount of "cliques" on campus can be intimidating to the shy computer information systems major, but don't worry, you will find your clique soon enough, and the social order will continue without a hitch. The social elite at Bentley can often be seen within the Greek organizations, but they are present in the varsity sports scene, as well. You may have to look hard to find people you get along with, or you may find your best friend on your floor freshman year; really, it's all about luck.

Hookups or Relationships?

Go to any party, and this question can easily be answered. There are lots of random hookups, mostly occurring under the influence, that will be forgotten (if need be) the next day. The smallness of the school can be virtually impossible to ignore if you want a hookup to remain a secret; there's no six degrees of separation here—try three degrees instead. Most people who are in relationships are involved with other Bentley students. This can be disgustingly cute in the early stages of relationships, when canoodling couples are seen holding hands on the way to class and kissing in the hallway.

Best Place to Meet Guys/Girls

Whether you are walking to class, checking out a book at the library, or ordering a beer at the Pub, you can find an attractive people anywhere on campus. The truth is, there is no one "main" place to meet guys and girls because the campus is crawling with beautiful people. That said, the pressure can be intense to maintain a certain level of grooming and upkeep in public, even for those dreaded 8:30 a.m. classes. When the pressure mounts, students head to the gym to attempt to stay fit and lean, making the elliptical machine a key spot to check out the opposite sex's goods. Because most dorm room parties will have a large number of familiar people, frat parties can be used to meet new people to randomly hook up with, yet they seldom lead to long-term relationships. If traditional ways of meeting people fail, just wait until spring when everyone is restless and ready to peel off the sweaters and lay out on the Greenspace in their new bathing suits.

Dress Code

A quick survey of a typical Bentley classroom will reveal a number of students who came to class "dressed to impress" in their Gucci suits or Armani pants, mixed in with those who prefer American duds like Polo or Ralph Lauren. You never have to worry about whether you think you're overdressed for class because, chances are, someone will top you. Many international students love the designer look, and any girl in the sorority DPhiE can be seen wearing Tiffany jewelry and outfits straight out of *Sex and the City*. If you want comfort, keep those sweats handy, but only wear them to the gym to avoid strange looks walking up the stairs. There are plenty of cliques on campus that continue wearing their Abercrombie uniforms from high school; however, chances are it's only a matter of time before they give in and buy a Prada purse or Burberry scarf.

Did You Know?

Top Three Places to Find Hotties:

1. Frat parties
2. Bars
3. Laying outside on the Greenspace

Top Five Places to Hook Up:

1. Frat parties
2. Off-campus parties
3. The library
4. Residence hall bathrooms
5. Dances

Students Speak Out On...
Guys & Girls

"If you are a girl looking for a guy, this is the perfect school for you. The ratio of girls to boys is roughly 60:40. And, yes, the guys are all really attractive."

Q "Bentley students tend to have **a lot of money, nice cars, and nice clothing**. I would say it's a good looking campus for guys and girls. If they aren't hot, they have money to do what it takes to be hot!"

Q "There are **a lot of hot guys** on campus."

Q "Most Bentley students are **pretty attractive**, and a lot keep in shape by going to the gym or just walking around the hilly campus."

Q "There are a lot of good guys who are fun to hang out with, but **girls have to search long and hard** for ones that don't have girlfriends."

Q "**Most guys here fit the same mold**. Girls are a little bit different; they tend to hang out in groups where they all dress and look alike. There are plenty of attractive people here, though."

Q "The girls here are really pretty, and **most of them are close to perfect**. The boys, on the other hand, I know the good ones are around, but I have yet to meet many of them."

Q "**The girls are great**, all 10 of them here."

Q "I have had a few different girlfriends since I have been here. There are a few girls here that are real nice girls and are down-to-earth. There is also a crowd that think they are elite and above the rest of the world. There is also a large crowd of them that dress very provocatively and can act as if they are very promiscuous, but they are actually just teases and end up being let-downs when you really get to know them! **The guys here are all over the spectrum**. Some are too rich and snobby, and others are like high schoolers for the rest of their life. Overall, though, there is a good crowd of down-to-earth guys."

Q "**If you are a girl, Bentley College will seem like heaven to you**. I am a female, and the ratio of guys to girls is approximately 60:40."

Q "**Everyone seems like rich, spoiled, preppy people** with too much money who only hang out in their cliques. There are not enough homely, down-to-earth kind of people."

Q "**Most people at Bentley are hot**. Lots of in-shape, healthy people who are smart and have a great mind for business."

Q "**Too many guys**. It's tough to find the girls on weekends because they go to all the upperclassman parties."

Q "There are **good-looking people everywhere**; everyone is in shape."

Q "The guys are not so hot, but we have some hottie athletes and a few cute frat boys. **I think we definitely have good-looking girls at this school**, which is good for the guys, but not so cool for us ladies."

The College Prowler Take On...
Guys & Girls

This is a campus filled with pretty people, and most of them know it, too. It's unfortunate, but the prettier girls do get stuck in the stereotype of being stuck up and high maintenance. There are always large groups of girls walking to class together, and it very common to remain friends with that same large group throughout your four years. The guys are generally laid-back in a social setting, but they can also be ruthless in a business meeting. Some frat guys get a bad rap of being pigs and preying on freshman girls, and while those guys do exist, not all males give off the shady vibe. However, once cliques are formed, it can be very hard to become friendly with someone in another established clique.

At parties, especially frat parties, the flirting and sexual innuendos can be taken to a new level. Combine good-looking people with unlimited amounts of beer, add them to a small space with loud music, and the recipe for disaster is inevitable. "Hooking up" on campus can refer to anything from making out to having sex, and caution is necessary when using this term when trying to be discreet.

The College Prowler® Grade on
Guys: B+

A high grade for Guys indicates that the male population on campus is attractive, smart, friendly, and engaging, and that the school has a decent ratio of guys to girls.

The College Prowler® Grade on
Girls: B

A high grade for Girls not only implies that the women on campus are attractive, smart, friendly, and engaging, but also that there is a fair ratio of girls to guys.

www.collegeprowler.co

Athletics

The Lowdown On...
Athletics

Athletic Division:
NCAA Division II

Conference:
Northeast 10

School Mascot:
Falcon

**Males Playing
Varsity Sports:**
290 (13%)

**Females Playing
Varsity Sports:**
167 (10%)

➜

Men's Varsity Sports:

Baseball

Basketball

Cross-Country

Football

Golf

Hockey (Division I)

Lacrosse

Soccer

Swimming

Tennis

Track & Field
(Indoor and Outdoor)

Women's Varsity Sports:

Basketball

Cross-Country

Field Hockey

Lacrosse

Soccer

Softball

(Women's Varsity Sports, continued)

Swimming

Tennis

Track & Field
(Indoor and Outdoor)

Volleyball

Club Sports:

Rugby (Men's and Women's)

Skydiving

Intramurals:

Basketball (Men's
and Women's)

Dodgeball (Coed)

Flag Football

Soccer (Men's and Coed)

Softball

Street Hockey

Ultimate Frisbee

Volleyball (Coed)

Athletic Fields

Baseball/soccer field

Getting Tickets

Tickets are not required for Bentley students to attend Bentley sporting events.

Most Popular Sports

In 2002, Bentley's field hockey team reached its first-ever NCAA Division II national championship, and the team has reached the national championship game consistently in the past several years. Women's basketball has had 10 appearances in the Elite Eight and holds a NCAA Division II record with 21 NCAA Division II tournament berths.

Overlooked Teams

Both the men's and women's rugby teams have been dominating their opponents in club play for the past few years; it won't be long before they are officially recognized as a varsity sport and are considered formidable players in their division.

Best Place to Take a Walk

Along the Charles River Parkway that runs under Moody Street.

Gyms/Facilities

Charles A. Dana Center

The Dana Center is the hub of athletic activity at Bentley. The first floor houses basketball, racquetball, and volleyball courts, a therapy room, saunas, a steam bath, a dance studio, a competition-sized swimming pool, and a separate diving tank. The second floor is filled with a fully-equipped fitness center.

Outdoor Tennis Courts/Baseball Field/Soccer Field/Track

Bentley is very proud of its new outdoor athletic facilities. The baseball stadium, which seats 1,700, is one of the finest collegiate facilities in New England, with two lighted fields, one synthetic.

Students Speak Out On...
Athletics

> "Varsity sports are big on campus. Contests and prizes are offered to students who attended varsity games. Intramural sports seem to be pretty big, but I don't really know much about them."

Q "There are **some teams that stand out**. There is a good crowd at most of the events. We have a super-fan program on campus that gets people to the events and gives out lots of free stuff. Intramurals are big, too. Over 50 percent of the people here are involved."

Q "**Intramural sports are huge here** and a lot of fun. Varsity sports are good, too. Football is the biggest. I know that I never missed a home game, and there are always fun activities beforehand, like tailgating parties."

Q "Sports on campus are somewhat popular. **Bentley has very strong sports teams**. Women's soccer and men's football have been awesome."

Q "**Varsity sports are pretty successful**. There is not really a big campus involvement, which is a negative. IMs are fun. A good amount of kids play basketball and flag football."

Q "**Varsity sports are semi-big**, but it depends on the person. Football games are huge because our football team is really good. Hockey is pretty interesting. I couldn't really be bothered to go see the rest. Intramural sports are fairly big, I guess I forgot to get involved with them, so once again, I don't really know."

Q "**The sports teams here are all Division II**, except hockey, which is Division I. They are all really, really good, especially the boy's football team and many of the women's teams."

Q "Varsity sports are a joke on campus. **Some of the athletes walk around campus as if they are amazing**, but everyone else, including many of themselves, know that it is not a big deal and that they are not going to continue on after college. A decent turnout of students to a sporting event only happens when they advertise to give out free tuition or a big TV or some other great prize."

Q "There are many athletes on campus, but I personally have never attended an event other than football. **Intramural sports are not that big** because the school does not give field time to intramural teams."

Q "Varsity sports are a big deal for the people playing them, but other than that, **school spirit is hard to find**. IM sports get big turnouts."

Q "Varsity sports seem to do very well against other colleges, but in popularity among students for game attendance, it seems that **they are practically paying us with bribes to attend their games**. So, it's not the central thing to do on campus."

Q "Sports are pretty big on campus; we're mostly Division II. **Men's ice hockey is Division I**. The college has a great IM program, too."

Q "Varsity sports teams are all very good but **don't have a big fan base, except for football**. Intramurals are competitive and fun."

Q "Sports are huge. **Bentley gives out tons of cash and prizes at events**, and you can tell that the people are really feeling it more and more."

Q "**For me, athletics are huge**. I mostly associate with just athletes. IMs are pretty big, too. A lot of frats are associated with IM sports and just students in general who didn't want to try and compete at the college level."

Q "Certain sports are bigger than others—football and field hockey especially. **IMs aren't huge**."

Q "**No one follows varsity sports here**. The teams are D-II, so no one cares, and the D-I hockey team plays off campus at a terrible arena. IM sports are completely unorganized."

Q "Intramurals and varsity sports are always the buzz around campus. There is **always some game to go to** and what not."

The College Prowler Take On...
Athletics

There is a harsh stereotype that exists at Bentley regarding student athletes: if a student is good in their sport, it means they would have never gotten into Bentley for their grades. Varsity athletes are not exactly taken seriously by the rest of the population, but are given significant leeway academically if a game or practice interrupts or overlaps into a class period. The football stadium isn't packed on the weekends with fans cheering wildly, but games are used as a way of "pre-gaming" for a party later on that night. The biggest up-and-coming sport on campus is hockey, which recently moved up to Division I play but is still struggling as it gets used to the tougher competition. In a few years, the Bentley/Army hockey game will be one hot ticket.

Devoted rugby club players are trying desperately to become a recognized team, but the interest shifts from year to year, and essentially, if there isn't one student dedicated enough to take charge, the club will disappear. Bentley simply is not a school you go to hoping to be drafted into any sort of professional sport, rather it has excellent high school athletes looking to continue their passion and stay in shape during their college years.

B-

The College Prowler® Grade on
Athletics: B-

A high grade in Athletics indicates that students have school spirit, that sports programs are respected, that games are well-attended, and that intramurals are a prominent part of student life.

Nightlife

The Lowdown On...
Nightlife

Club and Bar Prowler: Popular Nightlife Spots!

Club Crawler:

The club scene does not exist in Waltham, so students travel into Boston and its various neighborhoods to get their groove on. Given the large amount of college students in the city, the clubs are guaranteed to be packed Thursday to Sunday. Most clubs offer a discount on the cover charge if you're on the guest list—just call first to ask what the procedure is, since each club has its own promoters. The following are some of the best nightclubs the city has to offer.

Avalon

15 Lansdowne St., Boston

(617) 262-2424

www.avalonboston.com

Avalon is the perfect club to go to with a large group of friends. The dance floor is one of the biggest in the city. If you're used to the New York

(Avalon, continued)

or LA club scene, this is the place to be. Voted the number one nightclub in America and the most popular U.S. club. Avalon's "Avaland Fridays" are not worth missing. Occasionally used as a concert venue, Avalon is a must for any student to visit at least once.

Axis

13 Lansdowne St., Boston

(617) 262-2437

www.axisnightclub.com

This is a club purely for the true Boston area collegian. Two floors of complimentary-style music makes it a packed venue each night. The Friday night appeal is the techno scene downstairs on the large dance floor and the back to the '80s playing upstairs. The diversity of the Axis clubgoer always makes for an interesting night.

The Roxy

279 Tremont St., Boston

(617) 338-7699

www.roxyplex.com

A great club to take a date, the décor and vibe is a bit more mature and established than the Lansdowne clubs, but a good change nonetheless. The Roxy caters to a diverse population as it hosts "Chippendales" for the ladies every Friday and offers a reward card for frequent clubgoers.

Tequila Rain

3 Lansdowne St., Boston

(617) 859-0030

http://tequilarainboston.com

This nightclub extension of Jillian's is respected amongst the most faithful clubbers. You'll be coaxed in by the hottest top 40 beats, but don't worry if you weren't planning on clubbing because the dress code is sexy casual. With monthly and weekly events, such as Cuervo Nation, Buff Fridays, and wet t-shirt contests, there is a reason for everyone to go to Tequila Rain.

Bar Prowler:

What Waltham lacks in nightclubs, it makes up with in bars. Each local bar attracts students for a different night of the week, making it possible to go out each night with a sense of predictable fun.

Joe Sent Me

849 Main St., Waltham

(781) 894-3153

www.joe-sent-me.com/ body.asp

The Tuesday night bar to be and be seen at is Joe Sent Me, known simply as "Joe's" to Bentley-ites. Tuesdays are College Party Nights with 8 oz. $1 drafts. Thursday, Friday, and Saturday bring live music, and a newly opened patio could make Joe's even hotter. Don't expect a glitz-and-glamour décor here, but the spot is so

(Joe Sent Me, continued)

popular that is was chosen by one of the contestants on ABC's *The Bachelor* to watch her episodes a few seasons ago. The 21-and-over requirement is more relaxed on Tuesday nights, just make sure you're with a group of good-looking girls!

Mad Raven

841 Main St., Waltham

(781) 894-8188

www.themadraven.com

Although right next to Joe's on Main Street, the Mad Raven is typically the hang out for Brandeis students, and since Bentley and Brandeis students don't mix, you'd be hard pressed to find a Falcon in this joint on a regular basis. It's still worth while to check out, and who knows, maybe there's hope yet for Waltham collegians from different sides of town to bond over a good beer.

The Skellig

240 Moody St., Waltham

(781) 647-0679

www.theskellig.com

A traditional Irish pub in the front, a old-fashioned bar experience in the backroom. While the Skellig probably wasn't opened with the intention of being a college bar, it definitely knows how to show Bentley students a good time.

(The Skellig, continued)

Local bands play the backroom every Thursday night, the unofficial Bentley night, and most times, they are surprisingly talented. The 21-and-over law is increasingly enforced as the night goes on and more people want to get in.

The Wave Sports Pub

411 Waverley Oaks Rd., Waltham

(781) 894-7011

www.wavesportspub.com

The closest bar geographically to campus, the Wave is the newest addition in Thursday night bar hopping. A cover charge of $5 is sometimes collected, but there's always $1.50–$2 drafts, which make up for it. On Thursday's, the Wave is hit up for some early night pool before heading over to the Skellig.

Who's on First?

19 Yawkey Way, Boston

(617) 247-3353

www.whosonfirstboston.com

Right behind Fenway Park, Who's on First? is a Boston tradition. This sports bar is the place to be during the Red Sox season—it's usually pretty packed, but it makes for an incredibly fun atmosphere to take in a game.

Student Favorites:

Joe Sent Me

The Skellig

The Wave Sports Pub

Other Places to Check Out:

An Tua Nua

Embassy

Grendel's Den

The Kells

Margaritas

Matrix

T's Pub

White Horse Tavern

Bars Close At:

1 a.m., a few stay open until 2 a.m.

Primary Areas with Nightlife:

Allston

Brighton

Boston

Cheapest Place to Get a Drink:

The Wave

Favorite Drinking Games:

Beer Pong/Beirut

Card Games (A$$hole, Ring of Fire)

Century Club

Power Hour

Quarters

Useful Resources for Nightlife

http://thephoenix.com

www.boston.com/ae

www.bostonnightguide.com

What to Do if You're Not 21

The Backstage

Spruce Hall, on campus

(781) 891-2320

The Backstage, located in the basement of Spruce Hall, offers pool tables, foosball, air hockey, darts, and a free soda bar (but no alcohol). During the week, students can see bands, comedians, or even take part in some karaoke.

Copperfield's

98 Brookline Ave., Boston

(617) 247-8605

www.2nite.com/copperfields

The closest thing to being in a real bar without a fake ID needed (although you can try to use it if you want). No cover charge before 9:30 p.m. can be very appealing to poor college students on a budget. The bar has two floors and live alternative bands that play Thursday, Friday, and Saturday.

Jillian's

145 Ipswich St., Boston

(617) 437-0300

www.jilliansboston.com

Jillian's is a great place for those of drinking age (six full bars!), but even those under 21 can have a great time here. Above the first floor, Tequila Rain, is the giant arcade floor—a virtual indoor amusement park. From virtual bowling to basketball to skee ball to pool tables galore, this is one place sure to please everyone in your group. Most nights are 18 and over, but some Fridays and Saturdays can be 19 and over to weed out the college kids from the older high-schoolers.

Frats

See the Greek section!

Students Speak Out On...
Nightlife

"There are a fair amount of parties on campus. It's not out of control because we are a wet campus, and the school is pretty cool with allowing kegs to people who are over 21."

Q "**Parties on campus can vary and fluctuate**. The parties definitely depend on who's throwing them. Bars and clubs off campus are worth a look. However, make sure you bring a lot of your own friends, or else you are almost guaranteed a bad time."

Q "On the weekends, **you will find something fun to do**."

Q "There are **no frat or sorority houses** on campus, so most parties are small and in dorm rooms. Some good clubs in Boston that let you in if you're under 21 are Axis and Avalon, and Roxy on certain nights."

Q "**Parties on campus tend to be real crowded**. Not very many, if any, off-campus parties. Bars and clubs are 10 to 20 minutes away in Boston."

Q "Every Bentley bash is the same. Being near Boston, **there are so many clubs and bars to go to** that I have only even been to 10 percent of them, I bet."

Q "**The clubs in Boston are good**, but they can get expensive, and since everything shuts down at 2 a.m. or sooner, it's hard to get back to campus without paying a ton of money for a taxi. I recommend the Avalon, Axis, and Embassy."

Q "The parties here are really good; **we have a lot of fun**. There are tons of clubs and bars in Boston and a few in Waltham. I like Avalon, the Kells, Who's on First?, and the Wave."

Q "**The parties on campus are what a college party should be**. They are on campus, so they are not absolutely outrageous and wild, but they are exciting. They consist more of people who you know and have some form of a relationship with, even if it is minimal compared to some parties I have attended at other schools, that get so large that even the people hosting the party don't know half the people there."

Q "Parties are weak on campus due to the lack of fraternity houses. **On Friday nights, there are usually social gatherings**, but they are not fun unless you enjoy standing in a small common room sweating with 85–100 individuals drinking a beer. Saturday nights are usually dead, and no parties really go on during the week."

Q "Parties are pretty good, you can usually find one Thursday, Friday, and Saturday night. **Tuesdays are big bar nights**, but there's only a couple of bars in the Waltham area."

Q "**Parties are fun**. During the pledge process in the spring, the parties have been limited. There are tons of clubs in Boston, if you're into that, like Avalon and the Matrix. There is a bar that has Bentley night on Tuesdays in Waltham called the Wave. People also frequent Who's On First?, near Fenway in Boston on Thursday nights."

Q "The parties are average. **You can register a party when you are 21**, so the parties are legal as long as the people in the room are 21. The local bars are good, and there is a mix of good bars in Boston."

Q "**The parties on campus are dull and uninteresting**, unless you like lots and lots of beer pong. Off campus, the Boston nightlife is peerless. Maybe New York can compete, but I doubt it. Landsdown Street has the best DJs around, and there are tons of concerts in the area. Hundreds of dive bars in the area, and many upscale ones, make a trip to Boston on Friday night a must."

Q "Parties on campus are crowded and nothing special, but they usually aren't broken up by Campus Police. Students head to the local fraternity-run bar on Tuesdays, as **bars in Boston are strict on identification**."

The College Prowler Take On...
Nightlife

The party scene at Bentley can be overwhelming at first, during your first few months away from home. Everyone's "welcome back" parties will die down around mid-October, and then the midterm parties will start, concluding with end of semester parties. It's a sure bet that when going to an on-campus party, you will know at least half of the people there. Because frats don't have houses on campus, most Greeks will throw parties in their rooms. Dorm room parties are fun when you're a freshman—especially going to upperclassman rooms—but come sophomore year, the crowded beer-pong parties lose their appeal. The on-campus party scene can burn out any student come senior year, so the key is to get out and explore other college parties every once and a while.

Going to clubs in Boston can be an awesome time, but the only drawback is that, in order to make it back to Harvard Square to catch the last shuttle back to campus, you will have to leave the club early; a taxi can be expensive from Boston (around $35) but with a group of people, it is definitely worth it. An often disregarded city for fun is Providence, only 45 minutes away. Compared to Boston, Providence bars are a breeze to get into and perfect for the under-21 crowd. The big catch here is to make sure you have a designated driver!

B

The College Prowler® Grade on
Nightlife: B

A high grade in Nightlife indicates that there are many bars and clubs in the area that are easily accessible and affordable. Other determining factors include the number of options for the under-21 crowd and the prevalence of house parties.

Greek Life

The Lowdown On...
Greek Life

Number of Fraternities:
6

Number of Sororities:
4

Percent of Undergrad Men in Fraternities:
13%

Percent of Undergrad Women in Sororities:
13%

➜

Fraternities:

Alpha Gamma Pi
Alpha Sigma Phi
Delta Kappa Epsilon
Kappa Pi Alpha
Sigma Gamma Delta
Tau Kappa Epsilon

Sororities:

Alpha Phi
Delta Phi Epsilon
Gamma Phi Beta
Phi Sigma Sigma

Multicultural Colonies:

Delta Sigma Theta (sorority)
Phi Beta Sigma (fraternity)

Other Greek Organizations:

Greek Council
Greek Peer Advisors
Interfraternity Council
Order of Omega
Panhellenic Council

Did You Know?

TKE holds a **Monte Carlo Night** each fall during Homecoming for students and their families. Each spring, SGD puts on "Airband," an auction to bid on the first pick in the housing lottery and the first class registration spots.

Students Speak Out On...
Greek Life

"Only 10 percent of the campus is involved with Greek life, and the other 90 percent tends to like the people involved, but they laugh at the actual idea of joining a frat or sorority."

Q "Greek Life is **relatively small here on campus**. But during rush times, things are still crazy here."

Q "**There are active Greek organizations that sponsor different events,** but they do not dominate the social scene. There is not too much pressure to join a Greek organization."

Q "Greek life—**they seem like they think they're better** than everyone else."

Q "Greek life here is small. I wouldn't say it dominates the social scene, but **the frats throw the most bashes**. I hate Greek life, and I think it's stupid, and it's just there so people can buy their friends."

Q "Greek life doesn't dominate the social scene, but I know a lot of people who have pledged. **They throw great parties** (at least SGD does)."

Q "Definitely **doesn't dominate the social scene**, but it does play its role. During rushing time, fliers are everywhere, and people are pledging until all hours of the night. The frat parties are pretty fun."

Q "**Greek life is present** but does not consume the social scene."

Q "**It is a joke**. They are another group that segregates themselves from the rest of the community. They do not get involved with much outside of the Greek life programs."

Q "**Greek life sucks at Bentley**. There are a few fraternities and sororities, but nothing like any other college I have been to. Bentley does not have on-campus fraternity and sorority houses, so if this is of importance to you, don't come to Bentley looking for a big Greek scene."

Q "Greek life exists, but it's **not very popular**. Membership is small, and most people agree that you don't have to pledge to a frat or sorority to have friends and fun on campus."

Q "It doesn't dominate, but they have most of the biggest parties. It doesn't matter, though, because **you don't have to be part of the frat to go**."

Q "**Greek life is pretty popular**, but at the same time, the campus is so small that it makes the whole concept kind of redundant—why join a frat to hang out with people you probably will see everyday anyway?"

Q "**Athletes definitely run the show at this school**. There is a lot of Greek life; however, it is kind of a joke, seeing as there are no sorority or fraternity houses. They mostly just party in the dorms."

Q "**Greeks are a big deal up** until sophomore year, then everyone realizes how stupid they are."

Q "**Greek life is filled with meat-heads and idiot girls**. No fraternities or sororities are intelligent. They don't dominate the social scene."

The College Prowler Take On...
Greek Life

The Greek scene at Bentley, which by the way, is not ever actually referred to as "the Greek scene" by any student, is slightly untraditional when compared to other local universities. There are no fraternity or sorority houses on campus, and only a few frats have brothers who rent a house off campus for the purpose of having parties. With 13 percent of the student population in a fraternity or sorority, they are a visible force on campus, but mostly serve a social purpose. The events and fundraisers run by the Greeks are something to be proud of; however, their main function is to appeal to those who have a compelling need for sisterhood or brotherhood.

It's basically mandatory for every freshman, especially the girls, to check out frat parties during your first year at college. Frat guys will come to your floor and sell you tickets for the party and will run shuttle buses to the off-campus houses. After freshman year, the frat parties on campus are mostly Greeks and friends of Greeks only. Guys who aren't in frats will have a harder time getting into frat parties, but having a pretty lady on your arm can help.

The College Prowler® Grade on
Greek Life: C

A high grade in Greek Life indicates that sororities and fraternities are not only present, but also active on campus. Other determining factors include the variety of houses available and the respect the Greek community receives from the rest of the campus.

Drug Scene

The Lowdown On...
Drug Scene

Most Prevalent Drugs on Campus:
Alcohol
Marijuana

Liquor-Related Referrals:
481

Liquor-Related Arrests:
5

Drug-Related Referrals:
104

Drug-Related Arrests:
2

Drug Counseling Programs:
Alcohol and other drug prevention programs
Rhodes Hall
(781) 891-2947

Students Speak Out On...
Drug Scene

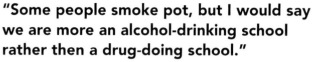

"Some people smoke pot, but I would say we are more an alcohol-drinking school rather then a drug-doing school."

Q "I'm not into the drug scene, so **I don't really know much about it**."

Q "**I hear about marijuana occasionally**, but nothing really more serious than that."

Q "**Drugs are not that prevalent** on campus. There are some students who smoke pot."

Q "If you want them, **you can find them**, but they are not overwhelmingly in your face."

Q "As far as I can see, **there aren't too many drugs on campus**. People do them, but they don't seem to be the biggest thing here. People would much rather drink at this school."

Q "**Drugs are accessible** but are not prevalent at parties. If people are going to do them, then they do it on their own or in small groups. They don't bring it to a party and do it there."

Q "**There is an abundance of marijuana on campus**, and you can pretty much call a number of individuals on any given night and pick up a nice bag. This is a big plus because there isn't usually much to do on weeknights other than get high."

Q "**Very little drug use on campus** compared to other schools. Mostly we are just an alcohol school. Some pot, but probably less than 10 percent of our college population uses it."

Q "Drugs here are **as prevalent as any other college campus**."

Q "The drug scene is much like any other campus, and far smaller than in some. **Campus Police crack down on anyone doing stupid stuff outside**, but if drugs are your thing, I'm sure you could get away with it, much like anywhere else. But if what you really want to know is how clean the campus is, I would say there is not that much of a negative influence."

Q "I know where they're at when or if I want them, but probably **the opportunities are pretty darn small** compared to most colleges. Then again, we're in New England, and we all smoke weed here."

The College Prowler Take On...
Drug Scene

If the Campus Police log is any indication of which drug is the most prevalent, it would appear there are a lot of stupid pot smokers who don't put a towel under their door and get busted not only for the smell, but also for possession. Alcohol use is widespread, and it's not highly uncommon for students to start drinking Thursday night and go until Monday night. The peer pressure to indulge can be stronger in larger cliques such as sport teams and fraternities, but if you choose not to booze, just be prepared to pitch in a helping hand when your roommates come back from a party and can't make it to the trash can fast enough.

As with most schools, it you want drugs, you will find a way to get them. Don't expect to be at an on-campus party and have someone offer you questionable pills or powder, because it won't happen. People either know there are drugs here or they don't.

The College Prowler® Grade on

Drug Scene: B+

A high grade in the Drug Scene indicates that drugs are not a noticeable part of campus life; drug use is not visible, and no pressure to use them seems to exist.

Campus Strictness

The Lowdown On...
Campus Strictness

What Are You Most Likely to Get Caught Doing on Campus?

- Cheating on exams or papers
- Drinking underage
- Destruction of campus property
- Parking illegally
- Making too much noise in your room
- Downloading copyrighted materials
- Hanging up unregistered posters in buildings
- Having too many people at an unregistered party
- Having drug paraphernalia in your dorm room

"**Drugs can be big trouble if you are caught. If you're drinking and are under control, or you are 21, you are fine. People who get in trouble are usually the people throwing the large parties.**"

"**Campus Police are very strict** about drugs and drinking if you get caught."

"They're not too strict. **They do their job**, but they also understand that we're in college to have fun."

"Campus Police are strict about drugs, but **they are somewhat lenient about drinking** on Friday and Saturday nights."

"It depends, really. **They are pretty strict about underage drinking in the Trees**, which are the freshman dorms, and really strict about drugs, especially when it comes to marijuana."

"They really aren't that strict here. It's not that hard to drink at all, but **they do have penalties for drinking** and are harder on drug violators than drinkers. Don't worry, Bentley is a party school!"

"Not strict at all. **They say you are kicked out for marijuana**, but nobody ever really does get kicked out for it. They just charge high fines for drug and alcohol violations, which is useless because it doesn't teach anyone a lesson or deter them from doing it again."

Q "Campus Police are not people you want to deal with. **They are trained to be intimidating**, and the majority of them are idiots. Avoid them as much as possible; they are very strict, and the school will fine the crap out of you for minor infractions."

Q "**RAs say that if they see it, they have to write you up**, but if they just hear about it, and you don't make it obvious, they let it slide. Cops are pretty 'anti-tolerance,' though—as usual."

Q "Campus Police aren't too bad, but some **RAs are a little strict**."

Q "Campus is not very strict. **Cops are laid-back**, for the most part, especially when you become an upperclassman."

Q "**Pretty strict, but they are also pretty cool**. I hurt myself once during a night of heavy drinking, went to Campus Police to get them to take me to the ER, and they were cool about it. I guess they figured I already learned my lesson."

The College Prowler Take On...
Campus Strictness

If Campus Police can help you out, they will. They always want to help you get out of potential trouble first; only if you talk back to them will you receive punishment. It's not an unusual sight for an officer to pull up next to a student carrying a 30 pack to their dorm and ask to see the student's ID. If the student freaks out and starts complaining about how his constitutional rights are being violated, chances are he will end up being escorted to the station and given a fine. However, if you do find yourself in this situation and are underage, don't be stupid and just accept the fact that you were caught. Give the officer the beer politely, and you most likely won't have to show them any ID, thus avoiding being written up, which can be worth the cost of the beer. The presence of Campus Police officers is hard to ignore, and generally, students like the idea of being safe and protected.

The idea of campus strictness can be viewed from another angle completely: the view from the classroom. The problems the campus has with students cheating on exams or copying papers has become an increasing concern to the administration. Their attempts to curb the problem include access for all professors to plagiarism software and newly created and enforced guidelines to convict a cheater. The crime is not to be taken lightly, as Bentley is constantly lauded in the media for having one of the first centers for business ethics in the country. The penalty for being caught cheating is almost as severe as being caught with an illicit drug—suspension and/or expulsion. The administration is still trying to work the kinks out of their new system, but until they do, cheating is not something the campus condones.

C

The College Prowler® Grade on

Campus Strictness: C

A high Campus Strictness grade implies an overall lenient atmosphere; police and RAs are fairly tolerant, and the administration's rules are flexible.

Parking

The Lowdown On...
Parking

Parking Permit Cost:
Free

Bentley Parking Services:
(781) 891-2201
www.bentley.edu/extranet/cp/ parking.cfm

Student Parking Lot?
Yes

Freshmen Allowed to Park?
No

Common Parking Tickets:
No Parking Zone: $25–$100
Fire Lane: $100
Handicapped Zone: $100

Parking Permits

Parking permits are free and readily available for upperclassmen. Pre-registration is required via MyBentley (*https://my.bentley.edu*) and decals are picked up at Campus Police headquarters. Special parking permits are available for guests and visitors at no charge.

Did You Know?

Best Places to Find a Parking Spot
Miller parking deck
Behind Rhoes and Forest in the afternoon

Good Luck Getting a Parking Spot Here!
Behind Collins Hall

Students Speak Out On...
Parking

> "Parking on campus is pretty bad. Freshmen can't have cars here, and Campus Police are very strict on ticketing. It's hard to find a spot on weekend nights."

Q "I think **there are just enough parking spaces for everyone** with a car, and it's not bad now that they opened a new parking garage."

Q "**It isn't very easy to park near the dorm buildings**."

Q "I think **the parking situation is good**. Many people complain, but that is because they are lazy. They won't be satisfied until they have a private spot outside their door. I do, however, have a problem with the fact that students can register two cars on campus; there is no need for a student to have two cars on campus."

Q "**The parking lots are poorly designed**, forcing the driver to back out of the lot if there are no available spaces. There are two parking garages, but they are designed similarly in a poor fashion."

Q "Parking is fairly easy. **The farthest walk from dorm to car is three minutes**, and people still complain."

Q "**There is an ample amount of parking** with the two new parking decks that have been added in the last three years."

Q "**Parking is tough to get close to your dorms**. However, it's free, and there are always spots somewhere."

Q "It's very easy to park if you aren't too particular about the location. **The campus is small, so worst case scenario is that you will have a three- to four-minute walk** to your dorm. If you are a commuter, however, the parking is fantastic, and there are lots of spaces close to the academic buildings."

The College Prowler Take On...
Parking

After constant complaints from the students over the lack of parking, two new parking decks were built within two years. However, many students feel the problem has not been alleviated and will only get worse as more and more people bring cars onto campus. Don't try being creative by creating your own parking space, because Campus Police will find your car and deliver a hefty fine for illegal parking. In fact, your chances of getting a parking ticket here are substantially greater than your chances of getting all As in one semester. People complain about getting tickets, but they often forget that parking is free—a rare feature in suburban colleges. The charge for parking privileges could be reality within a few years, leaving students with more to complain about.

The types of cars on campus have a dramatic range, from your grandfather's Oldsmobile to a Z (insert number here) BMW to a Hummer. The car you drive can be a symbol of your financial status if you want it to be; otherwise, we're all college students, and if it has wheels and a motor and can get us from point A to point B, no one will care what car you own. If you choose not to have a car on campus, the shuttle can only get you so far, so you better start schmoozing with your key-toting buddies.

B-

The College Prowler® Grade on

Parking: B-

A high grade in this section indicates that parking is both available and affordable, and that parking enforcement isn't overly severe.

Transportation

The Lowdown On...
Transportation

Ways to Get Around Town:

On Campus

Bentley Shuttle to downtown Waltham and Harvard Square

Schedules available at Student Info Desk

www.bentley.edu/extranet/ stulife/shuttle_service.cfm

(781) 891-2685

Public Transportation

Waltham Citibus

(781) 890-0093

www.128bc.com/waltham/ index.html

Mass Bay Transit Authority (MBTA), (617) 222-3200

www.mbta.com/index.asp

Taxi Cabs

Waltham City Cab
(781) 899-0303

Veterans Taxi
(617) 527-0301

→

Car Rentals

Avis
local: (617) 534-1400
national: (800) 831-2847
www.avis.com

Budget
local: (781) 890-3360
national: (800) 527-0700
www.budget.com

Dollar
local: (617) 578-0025
national: (800) 800-4000
www.dollar.com

Enterprise
local: (781) 894-6770
national: (800) 736-8222
www.enterprise.com

Hertz
local: (781) 642-0502
national: (800) 654-3131
www.hertz.com

National
local: (617) 661-8747
national: (800) 227-7368
www.nationalcar.com

Best Ways to Get Around Town

Grab a ride with a friend

Take the Shuttle off-campus

The "T" bus

Ways to Get Out of Town:

Airlines Serving Boston

American Airlines
(800) 433-7300
www.aa.com

America West
(800) 235-9292
www.americawest.com

(Airlines Serving Boston, continued)

Continental
(800) 525-0280
www.continental.com

Delta Air Lines
(800) 221-1212
www.delta.com

JetBlue Airways
(800) 538-2583
www.JetBlue.com

KLM
(800) 374-7747
www.klm.com

Midwest
(800) 452-2022
www.midwestexpress.com

Northwest
(800) 225-2525
www.nwa.com

Song
(800) 221-1212
www.flysong.com

United
(800) 241-6522
www.ual.com

US Airways
(800) 428-4322
www.usairways.com

Virgin Atlantic Airways
(800) 862-8621
www.fly.virgin.com

Airport

Logan International Airport
(800) 235-6426

Logan is 15 miles and approximately 30 minutes driving time from Bentley.

How to Get to the Airport

Knights Airport Limousine Service, (800) 822-5456

A cab ride to the airport costs around $40.

Greyhound

The Greyhound Trailways Bus Terminal is at South Station in Boston. For schedule information, call (617) 526-1808.

www.greyhound.com

Boston Greyhound Terminal
2 South Station
Transportation Center
700 Atlantic Ave.
Boston, MA 02110
(617) 526-1801

Amtrak

Amtrak has two terminals in Boston.
www.amtrak.com

Boston South Staion Amtrak Train Terminal
2 South Station
Transportation Center
700 Atlantic Ave.
Boston, MA 02110
(617) 345-7460

(Amtrak, continued)

Boston Back Bay Amtrak Train Terminal
145 Dartmouth St.
Boston, MA 02116
(617) 345-7958

Travel Agents

Regency Travel
206 Chestnut St., Waltham
(781) 891-8422

Travel Arrangement
336 Moody St., Waltham
 (781) 893-4747

Students Speak Out On...
Transportation

> **"Everyone here takes the Bentley Shuttle around. When you are looking to go into Boston, the Bentley shuttle drops you off in Harvard Square where the T Red Line is just a short walk away."**

Q "The Bentley Shuttle bus brings you around Waltham and also to Harvard Square, so **it's relatively easy to get around town**."

Q "Getting around is so easy. **We have a free shuttle around Waltham and to Harvard Square**, but after freshman year, almost everyone has cars."

Q "**The Bentley Shuttle bus takes students to downtown** Waltham and to Harvard Square in Cambridge. It's the best way to get around if you don't have a car."

Q "**Pretty good**. Buses go around a city loop and Harvard Square. Harvard Square is pretty popular."

Q "**Public transportation is great here**. There are many shuttles all the time to take you where you need to go in town or to Harvard Square."

Q "There is a shuttle-bus run by the college to Harvard Square. From there, **you can take the T anywhere in Boston** and access buses, trains, and the airport."

Q "**You can take the shuttle into town** or to the Boston subway stop, and you can get anywhere easily and for cheap. All around, it's easier when you have your own car."

Q "**Very, very convenient**. The shuttle is excellent, and it is being improved even further soon. It's only a 15-minute ride to Harvard Square, the center of the Hub."

Q "Pretty convenient. There is the Bentley Shuttle which takes you to various stops in Waltham, and to Harvard Square. It's also where you can **get on the T to get into Boston if you want**."

The College Prowler Take On...
Transportation

Within your first few weeks at Bentley, you will realize the importance of either having a car on campus or knowing someone with a car on campus. However, Bentley does provide several transportation options for students. The most popular services offered on campus are the free shuttles. One of the shuttles runs through downtown Waltham with convenient stops near popular areas, providing access to MBTA busses and the commuter rail train. The other shuttle is for Bentley students only, providing a direct link to get into Boston from campus via Harvard Square in Cambridge. From there, you are able to access the MBTA subway and buses to all points around the city of Boston. The shuttle ride from Bentley to Harvard Square is about 20 minutes and runs on a closely followed schedule, which makes it a fairly reliable way to get into the city. Students feel this feature sets Bentley apart from other local colleges. On hours when the shuttle might not be running, taxis are an option.

Cars are extremely common on campus and provide a little more flexibility for students. However, parking is and always has been an issue, and freshmen are prohibited from having cars on campus to prevent further overcrowding. For the unfamiliar driver, Boston can be a very complicated city to drive around, and street parking is fairly limited with garage parking being extremely expensive. There are many options for transportation that make exploring Waltham and Boston very accessible and easy.

A-

The College Prowler® Grade on

Transportation: A-

A high grade for Transportation indicates that campus buses, public buses, cabs, and rental cars are readily-available and affordable. Other determining factors include proximity to an airport and the necessity of transportation.

Weather

The Lowdown On...
Weather

Average Temperature:		**Average Precipitation:**	
Fall:	51 °F	Fall:	4.12 in.
Winter:	30 °F	Winter:	3.96 in.
Spring:	57 °F	Spring:	3.79 in.
Summer:	71 °F	Summer:	3.69 in.

Students Speak Out On...
Weather

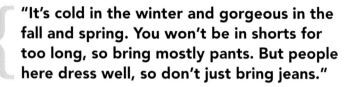

"It's cold in the winter and gorgeous in the fall and spring. You won't be in shorts for too long, so bring mostly pants. But people here dress well, so don't just bring jeans."

"The weather here is like the weather anywhere else in New England—unpredictable. The summers are hot, and the winters are cold. **In the fall, it can be 70 one day and 35 the next**. Bring all types of clothing."

"**The weather is typical New England weather**. Pack some of everything. You are bound to experience all the elements."

"It gets very cold in the winter (below freezing), so **you need a nice warm coat and a hat**. There are some warm days in early fall and late spring when you might like to have shorts."

"It's usually **cold all winter**. Bring lots of hoodies, boots, sneakers, winter hats, scarves, sweaters, jackets, and gloves."

"The weather is typical New England weather. **It is cold one day and hot the next**."

"The winters in New England are frigid. **Be prepared for snow**. You want to get a good heavy winter coat (Columbia makes excellent winter coats), probably some boots, and a lot of sweatshirts."

Q "It's New England. **Anything can happen**. If you don't like the weather, wait five minutes."

Q "It's typical New England weather—bring **all types of clothing** and maybe even a snow suit."

Q "**Boston is Boston**. If you don't like the weather, wait five minutes. If yesterday was freezing, today is T-shirt weather. Pack everything."

Q "**Pretty cold for most of the year**. It's New England, so obviously it's cold. September–October are pretty comfortable, and in April–May the weather is pretty mild, too. But winters can be pretty bad here. This one wasn't so bad; it was really cold, but not too much snow."

The College Prowler Take On...
Weather

Snow in April and shorts in November; two events not all that uncommon of the typical New England weather in Boston. Boston easily sees four very distinct seasons within the school year but with random days of other weather interspersed. Upon arrival to school in September, shorts and T-shirts are still common, but the change from late summer to fall can occur in an instant. The fall is a beautiful and comfortable time of year, with a slight autumn chill in the air and beautiful fall foliage. Winter is typically brutal, with a few months (about December–March) of freezing cold temperatures and an always decent amount of snow, meaning winter clothes are a definite necessity. Once spring finally begins to come around, the campus lights up, and people begin to reemerge from the woodwork and actually venture outside.

It is most certainly important to be prepared for all types of weather, from heat to rain to humidity to snow and everything in between. There are no surprises; it's typical New England weather here.

The College Prowler® Grade on
Weather: C-

A high Weather grade designates that temperatures are mild and rarely reach extremes, that the campus tends to be sunny rather than rainy, and that weather is fairly consistent rather than unpredictable.

Report Card Summary

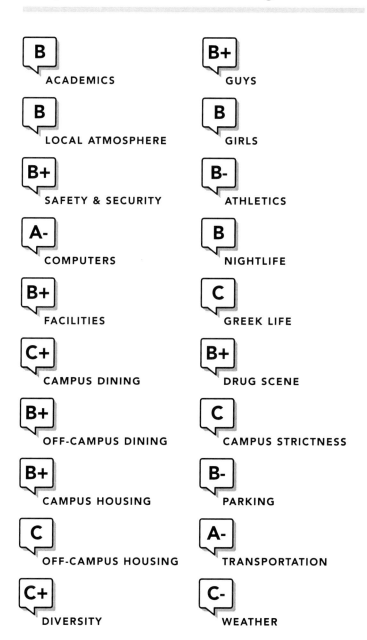

B ACADEMICS

B+ GUYS

B LOCAL ATMOSPHERE

B GIRLS

B+ SAFETY & SECURITY

B- ATHLETICS

A- COMPUTERS

B NIGHTLIFE

B+ FACILITIES

C GREEK LIFE

C+ CAMPUS DINING

B+ DRUG SCENE

B+ OFF-CAMPUS DINING

C CAMPUS STRICTNESS

B+ CAMPUS HOUSING

B- PARKING

C OFF-CAMPUS HOUSING

A- TRANSPORTATION

C+ DIVERSITY

C- WEATHER

Overall Experience

Students Speak Out On...
Overall Experience

> **"I have enjoyed my overall experience from Bentley thus far. I'm glad I chose this school."**

Q "Bentley has a real good image. It is getting better and better. Socially, you meet a lot of great kids. **Nightlife tends to get repetitive**, but if you go into Boston and other schools on occasion to switch it up, it's a good time. Overall, I like Bentley a lot."

Q I love it here! **Wouldn't change a thing**!"

Q "**I love Bentley** so much. I am so glad that I chose to go to school here."

Q "I enjoy it here, and I believe **I made the right decision**."

Q "I think **things need to be shaken up at Bentley**. Overall, the student body is pretty conformist and conservative. There is a strong Republican group. You won't find anyone with blue hair or a pierced chin at Bentley. There aren't many here with radical ideas, but you will find some promising entrepreneurs here and there."

Q "I love this school. It wasn't my first choice, but when I came here, **I felt so comfortable and I loved the people**. I am very happy I came here, and I wouldn't ever even think of transferring."

Q "I do not wish I was anywhere else. Not even a little bit. **I love this school**!"

Q "I am glad I chose Bentley. I would not want to be anywhere else. **You just have to remember to make the most of it** because it is over before you know it."

Q "I am not particularly fond of Bentley College. **If you are looking for a large social scene with many diverse students, don't come here**. The student body consists of primarily middle-to-upper-class white kids, and there is very little to do in order to entertain yourself on campus. I definitely wish that I would have visited more colleges before choosing Bentley because I wish I never came here."

Q "**School is okay**, I don't like the professors or classes, so I might look into transferring if it doesn't improve next year."

Q "**The facilities are great**, the education is great and not too hard yet, but the students need improving. I don't like the kinds of people that I'm meeting. Nice on the outside, but shallow or mean and racist on the inside."

Q "It is great! **A fun campus and top education**. I love it, and I don't wish I were anywhere else."

Q "I will often wish I were somewhere else; however, with my girlfriend here and having already made the commitment to be a businessman later in life, I believe **Bentley is the place to be**."

Q "**Academically, it has been great**, but socially, not that great."

Q "My experience has been awful. **The people who work for Bentley are not customer service oriented**. I went to a very large school for undergrad, and there, I never had this problem. Yet, at Bentley, I feel like a number not an individual."

Q "I love Bentley. I got into Northeastern, BU, Suffolk, and a few other schools in the area, and I had to choose Bentley. **The teachers are very friendly**, the workload gets tougher towards senior year, but the material is all extremely relevant to the real world. Go to Bentley if you want to know business, that's all there is to it."

Q "I like the friends I have made. I'm definitely not smart enough (nor rich enough—everyone here is loaded) to be here. I don't feel so alone, though, because a good majority of **the athletes are neither so rich nor so smart**. And there are lots of geeky kids who never partied or did anything other than play on their computers and read books. I would and would not like to be somewhere else. I'd like to be somewhere else because this really isn't a normal college experience; it's pretty lame. At the same time, though, I'm glad I'm here because I'm getting a practically free (really expensive) education, and I will most likely get a great job after graduating from here."

Q "**You have to be in love with business** to be entirely happy here, and it's not as close-knit as other schools."

The College Prowler Take On...
Overall Experience

The Bentley experience is hardly a normal college experience. From day one, you will be set off on a track to receive a unique business education. Hard work and effort are mandatory, but the rewards are endless. Students who are unhappy with their Bentley experience can actually attribute some of their issues to their own introverted-ness that keep them from exploring Waltham and Boston and the events, concerts, and meetings the school offers. Other factors, such as the disconnect in the concept of diversity and inability to form a relationship with local businesses, are out of control from a student perspective.

The opportunity to interact with professors who are leaders in the field, learn from renowned companies in the classroom, and have access to the latest technology is such a distinctive idea that Bentley is in a class of it's own as a business university. If you want to have a college experience that you can reflect back on and say you received an excellent real-world business education, were exposed to state-of-the-art technology, and had a good time while doing it, then your four years at Bentley will have been a success.

The Inside Scoop

The Lowdown On...
The Inside Scoop

Bentley Slang:

Know the slang, know the school. The following is a list of things you really need to know before coming to Bentley. The more of these words you know, the better off you'll be.

Bnews – The electronic posting community where students can buy, sell, or trade anything from books to concert tickets.

Discretionary – The extra money in your meal plan that can be used in the deli or coffeehouse when you don't have cash on you.

The Farm – The big parking lot on lower campus, usually where freshmen and guests are allowed to park without fear of getting a ticket.

GB – Any of the core business courses required.

Lower Campus – South campus, where Copley Suites and Orchard apartments are.

→

Ski lodge – The lounge area of the Student Center characterized by high ceilings and a fireplace.

Stu – The Student Center.

Up top – Usually refers to any academic area, either a classroom building or the library.

Things I Wish I Knew Before Coming to Bentley

- Meet as many people as possible during your first week.
- It's not a good school for people not committed to studying business.
- There is a large emphasis on group projects.
- Get out and explore Waltham as soon as possible.
- Learn to manage your time well.
- Don't call Boston "Beantown."

Tips to Succeed at Bentley

- Take an elective to balance out the heavy business course load.
- Research your professors before choosing your classes.
- Actually go to class.
- Don't wait to take your unrestricted electives until senior year.
- Do your homework yourself so you actually understand the material.
- Always dispute grades you disagree with.
- Don't get stuck doing all the work for a group project.
- Use your first two years to figure out what you want to major in.
- Know how AP credits can affect your class standing.

Bentley Urban Legends

Jay Leno went to Bentley! Well, he actually did for one semester, and then dropped out.

The original falcon statue in front of the library was stolen by Babson (our rival in business education) students because they are jealous of Bentley's academic superiority.

School Spirit

Despite being home of the Division II national field hockey champions and having division stars in the women's basketball and football teams, Bentley students are not oozing blue and gold. Because of the size, when students do watch a sporting event, they will most likely know at least one person on the team, and that is the main reason why they are there. The bookstore has started to carry more fashionable clothing bearing the Bentley name and has caused students to integrate them into their wardrobe. Chances are you won't hear someone say, "I'm so proud to be a Falcon!" but in their own apathetic way, they'll muster up a, "Yeah, Bentley is better than Babson," which is their way of saying, "Yay! Go Bentley!"

Traditions

Black United Body Fashion Show

Each Spring, the BUB fashion show showcases the hottest styles from local stores and boutiques. The music is kicking, and the models are flawless at this unique event.

Breakfast by Moonlight

On the night of the last day of classes each semester, BACCHUS organizes "Breakfast by Moonlight," an event featuring faculty and administration serving students breakfast around midnight. The price is usually $.99 with a canned good and $1.99 without a canned good, since it is used as a fundraiser (the charity changes each year). It's the only place you can catch the school president flipping pancakes alongside the vice president who is scrambling your eggs.

Business Bowl

An event for the true business student! Held each spring, students compete in teams of five on various real world business models and cases. Freshmen, sophomores, and juniors compete against each other, while seniors and graduate students go head to head. The teams have several hours to come up with the best solution to the business problems and then present their findings to a panel of judges. It is a highly recognized event in the local business community, and students are able to interact and network with business professionals, practitioners, and college administrators. Of course, cash prizes are awarded to the top teams in each class.

Greedy Bingo

This isn't your grandma's bingo! The entire campus literally packs the gym when Greedy Bingo is held once a semester. The prizes are extravagant and can be anything from a 50-inch plasma TV to courtside Celtics tickets to $500 cash to bicycles to fabulous gift certificates. Things can get intense if people are talking during the call, but usually is lightened as soon as "O-69" is called. Get there early to claim your card, and be ready to yell "Bingo!"

Midnight Madness

Just as the cold winter air is on its way out, Midnight Madness is there to welcome in the spring season. A night filled with games, food, and lots of competition, this event is primarily a chance for teams to go head to head to find out who the better tricycle or Big Wheels driver is. In order to participate, teams of about eight people are required, and the night is usually a big deal to athletes and fraternity members.

Monte Carlo Night

TKE puts on Monte Carlo night every Homecoming weekend. A chance for the ladies to wear that old prom dress one more time, this is an upscale, classy event. Alumni and parents are invited to attend and mingle with the fraternity brothers and other students while playing poker and bidding on high-end prizes. After going as a freshman, you realize it was a fun time, but freshmen generally don't attend every year unless they're in TKE or have parents that are alumni.

Spring Day

Get ready for a day filled with music, food, activities, and lots of beer while every student on campus congregates on the Greenspace for Spring Day; the last Saturday before finals start at the end of the Spring semester. As long as you and your guests (bring your friends from other local colleges along!) have wristbands and keep your alcoholic beverage in a covered cup, you will not be in trouble for drinking underage. If the idea of getting drunk at 9 a.m. isn't your thing, then enjoy the music (usually a totally rad '80s cover band), design your own trucker hat, or throw around a Frisbee. This is a guaranteed awesome time you won't forget.

Finding a Job or Internship

The Lowdown On...
Finding a Job or Internship

The Career Service office at Bentley is perhaps one of the most under-appreciated departments on campus. The staff is constantly making themselves available for resume critique and job search techniques while running various job fairs and workshops throughout the semester. Most students will find an internship or promising job lead with the help of Career Services.

Advice

Attend as many workshops and employer info sessions as possible in order to gain an idea of what type of internship you are interested in so that you can plan your academic courses accordingly. Make sure to register for Bentley's MonsterTrak Web site, where employers specifically post jobs for Bentley students.

Career Center Resources & Services

- Campus employment
- Campus recruiting
- Career fairs
- Career handout series
- Individual career advising
- Interview preparation
- MonsterTRAK
- Resume assistance
- Workshops, panels, and alumni networking events

Grads Who Enter Job Market Within

6 Months: 100%

Firms That Most Frequently Hire Graduates

American Express Financial Advisors, BAE Systems, Deloitte & Touche LLP, EMC Corporation, Ernst & Young, LLP, Fidelity Investments, Filene's/Kaufmann's, Goldman Sachs, Intel Corporation, KPMG, LLP, Liberty Mutual, Morgan Stanley, New York Life Insurance Company, Price Waterhouse Coopers LLP, Raytheon Company, Smith Barney, Staples Inc., State Street Bank & Trust, TJX Corporation

Alumni

The Lowdown On...
Alumni

Web Site:
www.bentley.edu/alumni

Alumni Office:
Lewis Hall
(800) 5-BENTLEY

Services Available

Online Directory

The online directory allows alumni to search for information on their old classmates.

Clubs and Chapters

In order to stay in touch with alumni if you are from outside New England, various alumni clubs and chapters are set up across the country and internationally so there is always a way to stay connected with Bentley.

Alumni ID

An alumni ID card is the way to receive the many benefits and services available for graduates. To receive your alumni ID card or alumni parking sticker, call the Office of Alumni Relations at (800) 5-BENTLEY.

Career Services

The Miller Center for Career Services is available to alumni no matter what stage of the job search process they are in. The resources, strategies, and opportunities such as skills workshops, networking events, and online job postings, are available to alumni for life.

E-Mail Forwarding

By establishing a free alumni e-mail account, you can take advantage of college e-mail services that include automatic message forwarding.

Insurance Discount

Bentley is partnered with Liberty Mutual to offer a special savings for Alumni Association members. The Group Savings Plus program provides a discount of up to 10 percent on the company's competitive auto and home insurance rates. The program also features 24-hour claims service, emergency roadside assistance to auto policy holders, and convenient billing options.

Major Alumni Events

The biggest events for alumni are homecoming and class reunions. Homecoming features the popular Monte Carlo night where alumni gamble and bid thousands of dollars away in only a few hours. Class reunions happen each year, and information is distributed to the alumni whose reunion year is approaching.

Alumni Publications

Alumni Update

Alumni Update is the official alumni magazine of Bentley College and is sent free to each alumni. It is published four times a year and offers news of campus, alumni events around the globe, and graduates' personal and professional lives. *Alumni Update* can also be accessed online.

Observer

Observer magazine, published twice a year, focuses on major college initiatives, faculty research, and students' work inside and outside the classroom. Class notes are also available for each issue to keep you in the loop on classmates' job changes, promotions, marriages, and growing families. Select graduates are profiled in the Alumni Notable profiles. The current issue can be viewed online.

Student Organizations

Allocation and Internal Audit Committee

Association of Bentley Activities

Association of Latino Professionals in Finance and Accounting

Bentley Asian Christian Fellowship

Bentley Asian Students' Association

Bentley Association of Chinese Students

Bentley Christian Fellowship

Bentley College Democrats

Bentley College Panhellenic Council

Bentley College Republicans

Bentley College Women's Center

Bentley Dance Team

Bentley Economics/Finance Society

Bentley Entrepreneur Society

Bentley Falcon Cheerleaders

Bentley Film Company

Bentley Investment Group

Bentley Jazz Band

Bentley Marketing Association

Bentley Model United Nations

Bentley Motoring Organization

Bentley Poker Club

Bentley Russian Club

Bentley Step Squad

Bentley Strategic Gaming Organization

Bentley Tae Kwon Do

Bentley Ultimate Frisbee Society

Best Buddies International

Beta Alpha Psi

Black United Body

Campus Activities Board

Capoeira Angola Club

Circle K

Commuter Association

Craze Dance Group

Freshmen Class Cabinet

Gamma Phi Beta

Graduate Association for Technical Analysis and Investment

Graduate Finance Association

Graduate Information Technology Management Association

Graduate Management Association

Graduate Marketing Organization

Graduate Student Association

Graduate Taxation and Financial Planning Association

Graduate Women's Leadership Organization

Greek Council

Habitat For Humanity

Hellenic Association

Hillel

Inter-Fraternity Council

International Buddy Network

International Students' Association

Junior Class Cabinet

La Cultura Latina

La Societa Italiana di Bentley College

Literary Society

Mathematical Sciences Club

Men's Rugby Club

Muslim Students' Association

National Association of Asian American Professionals at Bentley College

National Association of Black Accountants

Newman Club (Catholic Student Organization)

Organization of Hindu Minds

People Respecting Individuality and Diversity through Education

Racquetball Club

Residence Hall Association

Senior Class Cabinet

Ski and Snowboard Club

Skydiving Club

Society of Advancement of Management

Sophomore Class Cabinet

South Asian Student Association

Student Athletic Advisory Committee

Student Government Association

The Bentley Real Estate Group

The Vanguard

Vietnamese Students Association

WBTY – Bentley College Radio

Women's Rugby Club

The Best & Worst

The Ten BEST Things About Bentley

1	State-of-the-art technology at your fingertips
2	Up-and-coming reputation as the recognized leader in business education
3	Proximity to Boston and the free Harvard Square shuttle
4	Greedy Bingo
5	Real life experience many professors bring to the table
6	Ability to work with real companies in classes
7	Salary value of a Bentley diploma
8	Spring Day
9	On-campus concerts
10	The Greenspace on nice days

The Ten **WORST** Things About Bentley

1 Intense business focus

2 Cliques

3 Walking up the hill to class

4 Requirement to take (and pass) economics and finance classes

5 Science professors take themselves too seriously for being at a business school.

6 Parking

7 Group projects

8 Lack of recognition from Waltham businesses

9 Apathetic students

10 Construction and renovations all around

Visiting

The Lowdown On...
Visiting

Hotel Information:

Best Western TLC Hotel
477 Totten Pond Rd.
Waltham, MA 02451
(781) 890-7800
www.bestwestern.com
Distance from Campus:
2.4 miles
Price Range: $100–$130

Courtyard by Marriott
387 Winter St.
Waltham, MA 02451
(781) 419-0900
www.marriott.com
Distance from Campus:
2.6 miles
Price Range: $99–$189

→

DoubleTree Guest Suites

550 Winter St.
Waltham, MA 02451
(781) 890-6767
www.doubletree.com
Distance from Campus:
2.9 miles
Price Range: $159–$250

Hilton Garden Inn

420 Totten Pond Rd.
Waltham, MA 02451
(781) 890-0100
*www.starwood.com/
fourpoints*
Distance from Campus:
2.5 miles
Price Range: $89–$125

Holiday Inn Express

385 Winter St.
Waltham, MA 02451
(781) 890-2800
www.sixcontinentshotels.com
Distance from Campus:
2.6 miles
Price Range: $93–$150

Home Suites Inn

455 Totten Pond Rd.
Waltham, MA 02451
(781) 890-3000
www.homesuitesinn.com
Distance from Campus:
2.3 miles
Price Range: $119–$159

Homestead Studio Suites

52 Fourth Ave.
Waltham, MA 02451
(781) 890-1333
www.homesteadhotels.com
Distance from Campus:
2.9 miles
Price Range: $89–$169

Sierra Suites

32 Fourth Ave.
Waltham, MA 02451
(781) 622-1900
www.sierrasuites.com
Distance from Campus:
2.9 miles
Price Range: $80–$124

Westin Hotel

70 Third Ave.
Waltham, MA 02451
(781) 290-5600
*www.starwood.com/
westin*
Distance from Campus:
2.6 miles
Price Range: $109–$349

Take a Campus Virtual Tour

www.bentley.edu/vmap

To Schedule a Group Information Session or Interview

Call the Office of Undergraduate Admission at (781) 891-2244 or (800) 523-2354 to find a time and date that works for you.

Interviews are offered weekdays and selected Saturday mornings. In January, a limited number of slots are available by appointment, hourly from 9 a.m. to 3 p.m. During February and March, interviews are not available while the Admission Committee is reviewing applications. From April to December, interviews are available by appointment, hourly from 9 a.m. to 3 p.m.

Campus Tours

Tours are offered weekdays and selected Saturday mornings. Tours usually last for about one hour and can be scheduled with an interview together, provided there is availability in the schedule.

January 5–23: No tours offered since students are on winter break.

January 26–30: Tours offered hourly by appointment from 10 a.m. to 3 p.m.

February 2–March 26: No tours are offered with the exception of the week of Presidents Day (February 16) when tours will be offered hourly by appointment from 10 a.m. to 3 p.m.

March 29–December: Tours are offered hourly by appointment from 10 a.m. to 3 p.m.

Overnight Visits

Spending the night on campus can be arranged on an individual basis by speaking with the Admissions Office. You will be paired with a current student and spend a day in their shoes. You might go to a few Bentley classes, chill on the Greenspace, grab some dinner in the caf, and then stay up past midnight hanging out in the dorms. If an overnight visit if possible, it can be a great way to see the campus from a different perspective than simply a tour and information session.

Directions to Campus

Driving from the North

- Take Route 95/128 South to Trapelo Road, exit 28.
- Turn left at top of exit ramp.
- Follow Trapelo Road 2.6 miles toward Belmont.
- Turn right onto Forest Street.
- One mile on the left is the Bentley College entrance.

Driving from the South

- Take exit 27A—Totten Pond Road.
- At the end of the ramp, take a right and follow Totten Pond Road for 1.2 miles to the end.
- Take a right onto Lexington Street and go 0.2 miles.
- Then take a left onto Beaver Street; travel 1.5 miles (go around the rotary and continue on).
- Bentley College (and the entrance to the upper campus) will be on the left.

Driving from the East

- Follow Storrow Drive (west) or Memorial Drive (west) to the end and follow signs toward Arlington.
- Bear left at the sign that reads "To 16 S Watertown/ Waltham."
- Follow for .6 of a mile and turn right onto Belmont Street after passing the Star Market shopping center on the right.
- Continue on Belmont Street until it intersects with Trapelo Road.
- Bear right onto Trapelo Road and continue for 1.7 miles.
- Take a left at the light and follow the sign that reads "60 Waltham to Rte. 20." This is Waverley Oaks Road (Route 60).
- At the next traffic light, turn right onto Beaver Street.
- Continue on Beaver Street, which intersects the Bentley College campus. Turn right onto College Drive, just before the overhead pedestrian bridge.

Driving from the West

- Take exit 14 off the Massachusetts Turnpike.
- Follow signs to Route 95/128 North.
- Take Route 95/128 North to Trapelo Road, exit 28A.
- Turn right at the end of the exit ramp.
- Follow 2.6 miles toward Belmont.
- Turn right onto Forest Street.
- Approximately one mile on the left is the Bentley College main campus entrance.

Words to Know

Academic Probation – A suspension imposed on a student if he or she fails to keep up with the school's minimum academic requirements. Those unable to improve their grades after receiving this warning can face dismissal.

Beer Pong/Beirut – A drinking game involving cups of beer arranged in a pyramid shape on each side of a table. The goal is to get a ping pong ball into one of the opponent's cups by throwing the ball or hitting it with a paddle. If the ball lands in a cup, the opponent is required to drink the beer.

Bid – An invitation from a fraternity or sorority to 'pledge' (join) that specific house.

Blue-Light Phone – Brightly-colored phone posts with a blue light bulb on top. These phones exist for security purposes and are located at various outside locations around most campuses. In an emergency, a student can pick up one of these phones (free of charge) to connect with campus police or a security escort.

Campus Police – Police who are specifically assigned to a given institution. Campus police are typically not regular city officers; they are employed by the university in a full-time capacity.

Club Sports – A level of sports that falls somewhere between varsity and intramural. If a student is unable to commit to a varsity team but has a lot of passion for athletics, a club sport could be a better, less intense option. Even less demanding, intramural (IM) sports often involve no traveling and considerably less time.

Cocaine – An illegal drug. Also known as "coke" or "blow," cocaine often resembles a white crystalline or powdery substance. It is highly addictive and dangerous.

Common Application – An application with which students can apply to multiple schools.

Course Registration – The period of official class selection for the upcoming quarter or semester. Prior to registration, it is best to prepare several back-up courses in case a particular class becomes full. If a course is full, students can place themselves on the waitlist, although this still does not guarantee entry.

Division Athletics – Athletic classifications range from Division I to Division III. Division IA is the most competitive, while Division III is considered to be the least competitive.

Dorm – A dorm (or dormitory) is an on-campus housing facility. Dorms can provide a range of options from suite-style rooms to more communal options that include shared bathrooms. Most first-year students live in dorms. Some upperclassmen who wish to stay on campus also choose this option.

Early Action – An application option with which a student can apply to a school and receive an early acceptance response without a binding commitment. This system is becoming less and less available.

Early Decision – An application option that students should use only if they are certain they plan to attend the school in question. If a student applies using the early decision option and is admitted, he or she is required and bound to attend that university. Admission rates are usually higher among students who apply through early decision, as the student is clearly indicating that the school is his or her first choice.

Ecstasy – An illegal drug. Also known as "E" or "X," ecstasy looks like a pill and most resembles an aspirin. Considered a party drug, ecstasy is very dangerous and can be deadly.

Ethernet – An extremely fast Internet connection available in most university-owned residence halls. To use an Ethernet connection properly, a student will need a network card and cable for his or her computer.

Fake ID – A counterfeit identification card that contains false information. Most commonly, students get fake IDs with altered birthdates so that they appear to be older than 21 (and therefore of legal drinking age). Even though it is illegal, many college students have fake IDs in hopes of purchasing alcohol or getting into bars.

Frosh – Slang for "freshman" or "freshmen."

Hazing – Initiation rituals administered by some fraternities or sororities as part of the pledging process. Many universities have outlawed hazing due to its degrading, and sometimes dangerous, nature.

Intramurals (IMs) – A popular, and usually free, sport league in which students create teams and compete against one another. These sports vary in competitiveness and can include a range of activities—everything from billiards to water polo. IM sports are a great way to meet people with similar interests.

Keg – Officially called a half-barrel, a keg contains roughly 200 12-ounce servings of beer.

LSD – An illegal drug, also known as acid, this hallucinogenic drug most commonly resembles a tab of paper.

Marijuana – An illegal drug, also known as weed or pot; along with alcohol, marijuana is one of the most commonly-found drugs on campuses across the country.

Major –The focal point of a student's college studies; a specific topic that is studied for a degree. Examples of majors include physics, English, history, computer science, economics, business, and music. Many students decide on a specific major before arriving on campus, while others are simply "undecided" until declaring a major. Those who are extremely interested in two areas can also choose to double major.

Meal Block – The equivalent of one meal. Students on a meal plan usually receive a fixed number of meals per week. Each meal, or "block," can be redeemed at the school's dining facilities in place of cash. Often, a student's weekly allotment of meal blocks will be forfeited if not used.

Minor – An additional focal point in a student's education. Often serving as a complement or addition to a student's main area of focus, a minor has fewer requirements and prerequisites to fulfill than a major. Minors are not required for graduation from most schools; however some students who want to explore many different interests choose to pursue both a major and a minor.

Mushrooms – An illegal drug. Also known as "'shrooms," this drug resembles regular mushrooms but is extremely hallucinogenic.

Off-Campus Housing – Housing from a particular landlord or rental group that is not affiliated with the university. Depending on the college, off-campus housing can range from extremely popular to non-existent. Students who choose to live off campus are typically given more freedom, but they also have to deal with possible subletting scenarios, furniture, bills, and other issues. In addition to these factors, rental prices and distance often affect a student's decision to move off campus.

Office Hours – Time that teachers set aside for students who have questions about coursework. Office hours are a good forum for students to go over any problems and to show interest in the subject material.

Pledging – The early phase of joining a fraternity or sorority, pledging takes place after a student has gone through rush and received a bid. Pledging usually lasts between one and two semesters. Once the pledging period is complete and a particular student has done everything that is required to become a member, that student is considered a brother or sister. If a fraternity or a sorority would decide to "haze" a group of students, this initiation would take place during the pledging period.

Private Institution – A school that does not use tax revenue to subsidize education costs. Private schools typically cost more than public schools and are usually smaller.

Prof – Slang for "professor."

Public Institution – A school that uses tax revenue to subsidize education costs. Public schools are often a good value for in-state residents and tend to be larger than most private colleges.

Quarter System (or Trimester System) – A type of academic calendar system. In this setup, students take classes for three academic periods. The first quarter usually starts in late September or early October and concludes right before Christmas. The second quarter usually starts around early to mid–January and finishes up around March or April. The last academic quarter, or "third quarter," usually starts in late March or early April and finishes up in late May or Mid-June. The fourth quarter is summer. The major difference between the quarter system and semester system is that students take more, less comprehensive courses under the quarter calendar.

RA (Resident Assistant) – A student leader who is assigned to a particular floor in a dormitory in order to help to the other students who live there. An RA's duties include ensuring student safety and providing assistance wherever possible.

Recitation – An extension of a specific course; a review session. Some classes, particularly large lectures, are supplemented with mandatory recitation sessions that provide a relatively personal class setting.

Rolling Admissions – A form of admissions. Most commonly found at public institutions, schools with this type of policy continue to accept students throughout the year until their class sizes are met. For example, some schools begin accepting students as early as December and will continue to do so until April or May.

Room and Board – This figure is typically the combined cost of a university-owned room and a meal plan.

Room Draw/Housing Lottery – A common way to pick on-campus room assignments for the following year. If a student decides to remain in university-owned housing, he or she is assigned a unique number that, along with seniority, is used to determine his or her housing for the next year.

www.collegeprowler.c

Rush – The period in which students can meet the brothers and sisters of a particular chapter and find out if a given fraternity or sorority is right for them. Rushing a fraternity or a sorority is not a requirement at any school. The goal of rush is to give students who are serious about pledging a feel for what to expect.

Semester System – The most common type of academic calendar system at college campuses. This setup typically includes two semesters in a given school year. The fall semester starts around the end of August or early September and concludes before winter vacation. The spring semester usually starts in mid-January and ends in late April or May.

Student Center/Rec Center/Student Union – A common area on campus that often contains study areas, recreation facilities, and eateries. This building is often a good place to meet up with fellow students; depending on the school, the student center can have a huge role or a non-existent role in campus life.

Student ID – A university-issued photo ID that serves as a student's key to school-related functions. Some schools require students to show these cards in order to get into dorms, libraries, cafeterias, and other facilities. In addition to storing meal plan information, in some cases, a student ID can actually work as a debit card and allow students to purchase things from bookstores or local shops.

Suite – A type of dorm room. Unlike dorms that feature communal bathrooms shared by the entire floor, suites offer bathrooms shared only among the suite. Suite-style dorm rooms can house anywhere from two to ten students.

TA (Teacher's Assistant) – An undergraduate or grad student who helps in some manner with a specific course. In some cases, a TA will teach a class, assist a professor, grade assignments, or conduct office hours.

Undergraduate – A student in the process of studying for his or her bachelor's degree.

ABOUT THE AUTHOR

For those of who you made it through the entire book to get to this final page, congratulations! Now is your chance to read about the person who wrote the guide that may or may not convince you that Bentley is the school for you. As a marketing major, I held two different internships in public affairs and will soon be starting a career in public relations, hopefully with an agency in Boston. I have always enjoyed writing, for personal pleasure and as an integral part of my job function. The angle from which this particular College Prowler was written may be different than other guides because I was a second semester senior reflecting back on my entire college life. I wanted to write this book because as a senior, I felt I had the experience, knowledge, and resources available to me in order to offer you a complete and thorough look inside campus life. It was my goal to offer an unbiased, insider's look at Bentley and if I accomplished that, I hope to possibly meet some of you at alumni events!

This was a tough last semester of college for me, and if it wasn't for these special people, I couldn't have made it through with my sanity intact. Thank you, Dad, Eric, Adam, Sandy, Gram, Loren, Amanda, Lynn, and the Barneys. I love you, Mom.

Jessica Low
jessicalow@collegeprowler.com

California Colleges

California dreamin'?
This book is a must have for you!

CALIFORNIA COLLEGES
7¼" X 10", 762 Pages Paperback
$29.95 Retail
1-59658-501-3

Stanford, UC Berkeley, Caltech—California is home to some of America's greatest institutes of higher learning. *California Colleges* gives the lowdown on 24 of the best, side by side, in one prodigious volume.

New England College

Looking for peace in the Northeast?
Pick up this regional guide to New England!

NEW ENGLAND COLLEGES
7¼" X 10", 1015 Pages Paperback
$29.95 Retail
1-59658-504-8

New England is the birthplace of many prestigious
universities, and with so many to choose from, picking
the right school can be a tough decision. With inside
information on over 34 competive Northeastern
schools, *New England Colleges* provides the same
high-quality information prospective students expect
from College Prowler in one all-inclusive,
easy-to-use reference.

Schools of the South

Headin' down south? This book will help you find your way to the perfect school!

SCHOOLS OF THE SOUTH
7¼" X 10", 773 Pages Paperback
$29.95 Retail
1-59658-503-X

Southern pride is always strong. Whether it's across town or across state, many Southern students are devoted to their home sweet home. *Schools of the South* offers an honest student perspective on 36 universities available south of the Mason-Dixon.

Untangling
the Ivy League

The ultimate book for everything Ivy!

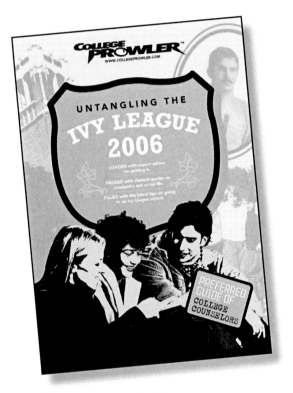

UNTANGLING THE IVY LEAGUE
7¼" X 10", 567 Pages Paperback
$24.95 Retail
1-59658-500-5

Ivy League students, alumni, admissions officers, and other top insiders get together to tell it like it is. *Untangling the Ivy League* covers every aspect—from admissions and athletics to secret societies and urban legends—of the nation's eight oldest, wealthiest, and most competitive colleges and universities.

Tell Us What Life Is Really Like at Your School!

Have you ever wanted to let people know what your college is really like? Now's your chance to help millions of high school students choose the right college.

Let your voice be heard.

Check out **www.collegeprowler.com** for more info!

Need More Help?

Do you have more questions about this school?
Can't find a certain statistic? College Prowler is
here to help. We are the best source of college
information out there. We have a network
of thousands of students who can get the latest
information on any school to you ASAP.
E-mail us at info@collegeprowler.com with your
college-related questions.

E-Mail Us Your College-Related Questions!

Check out ***www.collegeprowler.com*** for more details.
1-800-290-2682

Write For Us!
Get published! Voice your opinion.

Writing a College Prowler guidebook is both fun and rewarding; our open-ended format allows your own creativity free reign. Our writers have been featured in national newspapers and have seen their names in bookstores across the country. Now is your chance to break into the publishing industry with one of the country's fastest-growing publishers!

Apply now at ***www.collegeprowler.com***

Contact editor@collegeprowler.com or
call 1-800-290-2682 for more details.

Pros and Cons

Still can't figure out if this is the right school for you?
You've already read through this in-depth guide; why not
list the pros and cons? It will really help with narrowing down
your decision and determining whether or not
this school is right for you.

Pros	Cons
....	....
....	....
....	....
....	....
....	....
....	....
....	....
....	....
....	....
....	....
....	....
....	....
....	....

Pros and Cons

Still can't figure out if this is the right school for you?
You've already read through this in-depth guide; why not
list the pros and cons? It will really help with narrowing down
your decision and determining whether or not
this school is right for you.

Pros	Cons
....	....
....	....
....	....
....	....
....	....
....	....
....	....
....	....
....	....
....	....
....	....
....	....
....	....

Notes

....

....

....

....

....

....

....

....

....

....

....

....

....

....

Notes

....

....

....

....

....

....

....

....

....

....

....

....

....

....

Notes

Notes

....

....

....

....

....

....

....

....

....

....

....

....

....

Notes

Notes

....

....

....

....

....

....

....

....

....

....

....

....

....

Notes

....

....

....

....

....

....

....

....

....

....

....

....

....

Notes

Notes

Notes

....

....

....

....

....

....

....

....

....

....

....

....

....

....

Notes

....

....

....

....

....

....

....

....

....

....

....

....

....

Notes

....

....

....

....

....

....

....

....

....

....

....

....

....

Notes

....

....

....

....

....

....

....

....

....

....

....

....

....

....

Notes

···

···

···

···

···

···

···

···

···

···

···

···

···

Notes

....

....

....

....

....

....

....

....

....

....

....

....

....

....

Notes

....

....

....

....

....

....

....

....

....

....

....

....

....

Notes

....

....

....

....

....

....

....

....

....

....

....

....

....

Notes

....

....

....

....

....

....

....

....

....

....

....

....

....

....

Notes

....

....

....

....

....

....

....

....

....

....

....

....

....

Notes

....

....

....

....

....

....

....

....

....

....

....

....

....

Notes

....

....

....

....

....

....

....

....

....

....

....

....

....

Notes

....

....

....

....

....

....

....

....

....

....

....

....

....